WAR

II

SAMMY FRANCO

Also by Sammy Franco

1001 Street Fighting Secrets: The Principles of Contemporary Fighting Arts
Combat Pressure Points
Cane Fighting
Double End Bag Training
The Heavy Bag Bible
The Widow Maker Compendium
Invincible: Mental Toughness Techniques for Peak Performance
Unleash Hell: A Step-by-Step Guide to Devastating Widow Maker Combinations
Feral Fighting: Advanced Widow Maker Fighting Techniques
The Widow Maker Program: Extreme Self-Defense for Deadly Force Situations
Savage Street Fighting: Tactical Savagery as a Last Resort
Heavy Bag Combinations
Heavy Bag Training
The Complete Body Opponent Bag Book
Stand and Deliver: A Street Warrior's Guide to Tactical Combat Stances
Maximum Damage: Hidden Secrets Behind Brutal Fighting Combinations
First Strike: End a Fight in Ten Seconds or Less
The Bigger They Are, The Harder They Fall
Self-Defense Tips and Tricks
Kubotan Power: Quick & Simple Steps to Mastering the Kubotan Keychain
Gun Safety: For Home Defense and Concealed Carry
Out of the Cage: A Guide to Beating a Mixed Martial Artist on the Street
Warrior Wisdom: Inspiring Ideas from the World's Greatest Warriors
War Machine: How to Transform Yourself Into a Vicious Street Fighter
When Seconds Count: Self-Defense for the Real World
Killer Instinct: Unarmed Combat for Street Survival
Street Lethal: Unarmed Urban Combat

War Machine II: Real-World Self-Defense Skills for The Warrior Within
Copyright © 2023 by Sammy Franco
ISBN: 978-1-941845-79-0
Printed in the United States of America
Visit online at: ContemporaryFightingArts.com

This one is for Fonto.
My loyal and regal companion.
You will never be forgotten.

Contents

"Victory at all costs, victory in spite of all terror, victory however long and hard the road may be; for without victory there is no survival."

– Winston Churchill

Disclaimer

The author, publisher, and distributors of this book will accept no responsibility, nor are they liable to any person or entity whatsoever for any injury, damage, or loss of any sort that may arise out of practicing, teaching, or disseminating of any techniques or ideas contained herein.

You assume full responsibility for the use of the information in this book and agree that the author, distributor and contributors hold no liability to you for claims, damages, costs and expenses, legal fees, or any other costs incurred due to or in any way related to your reliance on anything derived from this book or its contents.

Additionally, it is the reader's responsibility to research and comply with all local, state, and federal laws and regulations pertaining to the possession, carry, and use of self-defense weapons. This book is for educational reference information only!

Before you begin any exercise or activity, including those suggested in this book, it is important to check with your physician to see if you have any condition that might be aggravated by strenuous training. The information contained in this book is not designed to diagnose, treat, or manage any physical health conditions.

Welcome Back

Welcome back to the War Machine program. I assume that by now you have read my first book in the series entitled, *War Machine: How to Transform Yourself into a Vicious and Deadly Street Fighter.* If not, I encourage you to study it before launching forward with this advanced book. And for those of you who have already read the book, congratulations are in order.

So now you've decided to take the next step by purchasing **War Machine II**. Excellent choice. This oversized book introduces you to the vast array of street combat tactics for real-world self-defense. I've made certain that no stone was left unturned by providing you with the most cutting-edge fighting tactics of our time.

War Machine II is divided into eight chapters. Each one covers a critical element of real-world combatives.

Chapter One explains the structural weaknesses of the human anatomy and the medical implications associated with it. Here, you'll learn what it takes to take a vicious criminal adversary out of commission during a crisis self-defense situation. This chapter also includes a detailed list of ineffective striking targets promulgated in most martial arts/ self-defense schools.

Chapter Two gives you a complete and thorough understanding of the natural body weapons (NBW). Here you'll see how each of these devastating self-defense techniques are put to use during an emergency combat situation.

Chapter Three is all about offense skills and techniques. It also includes (20) twenty efficient and brutal fighting combinations that you can seamlessly add to your repertoire.

Chapter Four gives you the knowledge, skills and attitude

necessary to handle most ground fighting situations. Topics include: the five ground fighting positions, the inherent risks and limitations of some submission tactics, effective street submission techniques, how to maintain a low base from the mount, the pummel, finger breaking tactics, crushing tactics, biting and gouging skills, escape from the mount, guard and perpendicular positions, hand grips, anatomical handles, the tail spin technique, training tips and suggestions.

Chapter Five covers how to escape from just about every conceivable grab, choke and hold from the stand-up position. Step by step photos show you escapes from two-hand wrist grabs (high and low), one hand wrist grabs, front shirt grabs, two hand throat choke, side shirt grab, rear bear hug (arms free and pinned to sides), rear collar grab, rear forearm choke, side head lock, finger in the face, front bear hug (arms free), shoulder drape and chest poke.

Chapter Six is about defense. Here, I'll cover the fighting stance, natural stance, de-escalation stances, knife defense stance, bludgeon defense stance, range proficiency, understanding the clinch, clinching for defense, controlling the clinch, fighting in the clinch, mobility and footwork, blocking techniques, limited application of the cross block, avoiding the latest trends and gimmicks, and how to take a punch.

Defending against multiple attackers is a difficult and treacherous task, but you can survive such a confrontation by applying the strategic tactics and techniques found in Chapter Seven. Here you'll learn about escape routes, makeshift weapons, tactical footwork, determining the *alpha* in the group, the human shield principle, attack skills, and much more.

The serious self-defense practitioner thinks nothing of spending countless hours conditioning and preparing for a possible criminal street assault. However, very few are adequately prepared to handle a criminal intruder in their home. Chapter Eight covers planning for a home intrusion, contacting the cops, building a *safe room*, holding a criminal at gunpoint, saving the evidence, post traumatic syndrome, criminal awareness skills, and more tips and strategies to keep you and your loved ones safe.

Chapter Nine has over two-hundred safety rules and guidelines that will help you avoid becoming a victim of street crime. Topics include: automotive safety, street survival tips, child safety, home security, workplace safety, and vacation and travel precautions.

At the end of the book, I've also included the War Machine code of conduct, glossary of terminology, and suggested reading and viewing.

I also encourage you to read this book from beginning to end, chapter by chapter. Only after you have read the entire book should you treat it as a reference and skip around, reading those chapters that directly apply to your specific circumstance.

Finally, the material contained in this book is not designed for sport combat or tournament competitions. The information and techniques contained herein are dangerous and should only be used to protect yourself or a loved one from the immediate risk of unlawful attack.

Remember, the decision to employ physical force must always be a last resort, after all other means of avoiding violence has been thoroughly exhausted.

Walk in peace.

Sammy Franco
ContemporaryFightingArts.com

INTRODUCTION
Contemporary Fighting Arts

Exploring Contemporary Fighting Arts

Before diving head first into this book, I'd like to first introduce you to my unique system of fighting, Contemporary Fighting Arts (CFA). I hope it will give you a greater understanding and appreciation of the material covered in this book. And for those of you who are already familiar with my CFA system, you can skip to chapter one.

Contemporary Fighting Arts® (CFA), is a state-of-the-art combat system that was introduced to the world in 1983. This sophisticated and practical system of self-defense is designed specifically to provide efficient and effective methods to avoid, defuse, confront, and neutralize both armed and unarmed assailants in a variety of deadly situations and circumstances.

Unlike karate, kung-fu, mixed martial arts and the like, CFA is the first offensive-based American martial art that is specifically designed for the violence that plagues our cruel city streets. CFA dispenses with the extraneous and the impractical and focuses on real-life street fighting.

Every technique and tactic found within the CFA system must meet three essential criteria for fighting: efficiency, effectiveness, and safety. Efficiency means that the techniques permit you to reach your combative objective quickly and economically. Effectiveness means that the elements of the system will produce the desired effect. Finally, Safety means that the combative elements provide the least amount of danger and risk for you - the fighter.

CFA is not about tournaments or senseless competition. It doesn't require you to waste time and energy practicing forms (katas) or other impractical rituals. There are no theatrical kicks or exotic techniques. Finally, CFA doesn't adhere blindly to tradition for tradition's sake. Simply put, it's a scientific yet pragmatic approach to staying alive on the streets.

CFA has been taught to people of all walks of life. Some include the U.S. Border Patrol, police officers, deputy sheriffs, security guards, military personnel, private investigators, surgeons, lawyers, college professors, airline pilots, as well as black belts, boxers, and kick boxers. CFA's broad appeal results from its ability to teach people how to really fight.

It's All In The Name

Before discussing the three components that make up Contemporary Fighting Arts, it is important to understand how CFA acquired its unique name. To begin, the first word, "Contemporary," was selected because it refers to the system's modern, up-to-date orientation. Unlike traditional martial arts, CFA is specifically designed to meet the challenges of our modern world.

The second term, "Fighting," was chosen because it accurately describes the system's combat orientation. After all, why not just call it Contemporary Martial Arts? There are two reasons for this. First, the word "martial" conjures up images of traditional and impractical martial art forms that are antithetical to the system. Second, why dilute a perfectly functional name when the word "fighting" defines the system so succinctly? Contemporary Fighting Arts is about teaching people how to really fight.

Let's look at the last word, "Arts." In the subjective sense, "art" refers to the combat skills that are acquired through arduous study, practice, and observation. The bottom line is that effective street fighting skills will require consistent practice and attention. Take, for example, something as seemingly basic as an elbow strike, which will actually require hundreds of hours of practice to perfect.

The pluralization of the word "Art" reflects CFA's protean instruction. The various components of CFA's training (i.e., firearms training, stick fighting, ground fighting, natural body weapon mastery, and so on) have all truly earned their status as individual art forms and, as such, require years of consistent study and practice to perfect. To acquire a greater understanding of CFA, here is an overview of the system's three vital components: the physical, the mental, and the spiritual.

The Physical Component

The physical component of CFA focuses on the physical development of a fighter, including physical fitness, weapon and technique mastery, and self-defense attributes.

Physical Fitness

If you are going to prevail in a street fight, you must be physically fit. It's that simple. In fact, you will never master the tools and skills of combat unless you're in excellent physical shape. On the average, you will have to spend more than an hour a day to achieve maximum fitness.

In CFA physical fitness comprises the following three broad

components: cardiorespiratory conditioning, muscular/skeletal conditioning, and proper body composition.

The cardiorespiratory system includes the heart, lungs, and circulatory system, which undergo tremendous stress during the course of a street fight. So you're going to have to run, jog, bike, swim, or skip rope to develop sound cardiorespiratory conditioning. Each aerobic workout should last a minimum of 30 minutes and be performed at least four times per week.

The second component of physical fitness is muscular/ skeletal conditioning. In the streets, the strong survive and the rest go to the morgue. To strengthen your bones and muscles to withstand the rigors of a real fight, your program must include progressive resistance (weight training) and calisthenics. You will also need a stretching program designed to loosen up every muscle group. You can't kick, punch, ground fight, or otherwise execute the necessary body mechanics if you're "tight" or inflexible. Stretching on a regular basis will also increase the muscles' range of motion, improve circulation, reduce the possibility of injury, and relieve daily stress.

The final component of physical fitness is proper body composition: simply, the ratio of fat to lean body tissue. Your diet and training regimen will affect your level or percentage of body fat significantly. A sensible and consistent exercise program accompanied by a healthy and balanced diet will facilitate proper body composition. Do not neglect this important aspect of physical fitness.

Weapon and Technique Mastery

You won't stand a chance against a vicious assailant if you don't master the techniques of fighting. In CFA, we teach our students both armed and unarmed methods of combat. Unarmed fighting requires that you master a complete arsenal of natural body weapons and techniques. In conjunction, you must also learn the various stances, hand positioning, footwork, body mechanics, defensive structure, locks, chokes, and various holds. Keep in mind that something as simple as a basic punch will actually require hundreds of hours to perfect.

Range proficiency is another important aspect of weapon and technique mastery. Briefly, range proficiency is the ability to fight effectively in all three ranges of unarmed fighting. Although punching range tools are emphasized in CFA, kicking and grappling ranges cannot be neglected. Our kicking range tools consist of deceptive and powerful low-line kicks. Grappling range tools include head-butts, elbows, knees, foot stomps, biting, tearing, gouging, and crushing tactics.

Although CFA focuses on striking, we also teach our students a myriad of chokes, locks, and holds that can be used in a ground fight. While such grappling range submission techniques are not the most preferred methods of dealing with a ground fighting situation, they must be developed.

Defensive tools and skills are also taught. Our defensive structure is efficient, uncomplicated, and impenetrable. It provides the fighter maximum protection while allowing complete freedom of choice for acquiring offensive control. Our defensive structure is based on distance, parrying, blocking, evading, mobility, and stance structure. Simplicity is always the key.

Students are also instructed in specific methods of armed fighting. For example, CFA provides instruction about firearms for personal and household protection. We provide specific guidelines for handgun purchasing, operation, nomenclature, proper caliber, shooting fundamentals, cleaning, and safe storage. Our firearm program also focuses on owner responsibility and the legal ramifications regarding the use of deadly force.

CFA's weapons program also consists of natural body weapons, knives and edged weapons, single and double stick, makeshift weaponry, the side-handle baton, and oleoresin capsicum (OC) spray.

Combat Attributes

Your offensive and defensive tools are useless unless they are used strategically. For any tool or technique to be effective in a real fight, it must be accompanied by specific attributes. Attributes are qualities that enhance a particular tool, technique, or maneuver. Some examples include speed, power, timing, coordination, accuracy, non-telegraphic movement, balance, and target orientation.

CFA also has a wide variety of training drills and methodologies designed to develop and sharpen these combat attributes. For example, our students learn to ground fight while blindfolded, spar with one arm tied down, and fight while handcuffed.

Reality is the key. For example, in class students participate in full-contact drills against fully padded assailants, and real weapon disarms are rehearsed and analyzed in a variety of dangerous scenarios. Students also train with a large variety of equipment, including heavy bags, double-end bags, uppercut bags, pummel bags, focus mitts, striking shields, mirrors, rattan sticks, training bats, kicking pads, knife drones, trigger-sensitive (mock) guns, full-body armor, and numerous environmental props.

There are more than two hundred unique training methodologies used in Contemporary Fighting Arts. Each one is scientifically designed to prepare students for the hard-core realities of real world combat. There are also three specific training methodologies used to develop and sharpen the fundamental attributes and skills of armed and unarmed fighting, including proficiency training, conditioning training, and street training.

Proficiency training can be used for both armed and unarmed skills. When conducted properly, proficiency training develops speed, power, accuracy, non-telegraphic movement, balance, and general psychomotor skill. The training objective is to sharpen one specific body weapon, maneuver, or technique at a time by executing it over and over for a prescribed number of repetitions. Each time the technique or maneuver is executed with "clean" form at various speeds. Movements are also performed with the eyes closed to develop a kinesthetic "feel" for the action. Proficiency training can be accomplished through the use of various types of equipment, including the heavy bag, double-end bag, focus mitts, training knives, real and mock pistols, striking shields, shin and knee guards, foam and plastic bats, mannequin heads, and so on.

Conditioning training develops endurance, fluidity, rhythm, distancing, timing, speed, footwork, and balance. In most cases, this type of training requires the student to deliver a variety of fighting combinations for three- or four-minute rounds separated by 30-second breaks. Like proficiency training, this type of training can also be performed at various speeds. A good workout consists of at least five rounds. Conditioning training can be performed on the bags with full-contact sparring gear, rubber training knives, focus mitts, kicking shields, and shin guards, or against imaginary assailants in shadow fighting.

Conditioning training is not necessarily limited to just three-

or four-minute rounds. For example, CFA's ground fighting training can last as long as 30 minutes. The bottom line is that it all depends on what you are training for.

Street training is the final preparation for the real thing. Since many violent altercations are explosive, lasting an average of 20 seconds, you must prepare for this possible scenario. This means delivering explosive and powerful compound attacks with vicious intent for approximately 20 seconds, resting one minute, and then repeating the process.

Street training prepares you for the stress and immediate fatigue of a real fight. It also develops speed, power, explosiveness, target selection and recognition, timing, footwork, pacing, and breath control. You should practice this methodology in different lighting, on different terrains, and in different environmental settings. You can use different types of training equipment as well. For example, you can prepare yourself for multiple assailants by having your training partners attack you with focus mitts from a variety of angles, ranges, and target postures. For 20 seconds, go after them with low-line kicks, powerful punches, and devastating strikes.

When all is said and done, the physical component creates a fighter who is physically fit and armed with an arsenal of techniques that can be deployed with destructive results.

The Mental Component

The mental component of CFA focuses on the cerebral aspects of a fighter, developing killer instinct, strategic/tactical awareness, analysis and integration skills, philosophy, and cognitive skills.

The Killer Instinct

Deep within each of us is a cold and deadly primal power known as the "killer instinct." The killer instinct is a vicious combat mentality that surges to your consciousness and turns you into a fierce fighter who is free of fear, anger, and apprehension. If you want to survive the horrifying dynamics of real criminal violence, you must cultivate and utilize this instinctive killer mentality.

Visualization and crisis rehearsal are just two techniques used to develop, refine, and channel this extraordinary source of strength and energy so that it can be used to its full potential.

Strategic/Tactical Awareness

Strategy is the bedrock of preparedness. In CFA, there are three unique categories of strategic awareness that will diminish the likelihood of criminal victimization. They are criminal awareness, situational awareness, and self-awareness. When developed, these essential skills prepare you to assess a wide variety of threats instantaneously and accurately. Once you've made a proper threat assessment, you will be able to choose one of the following five self-defense options: comply, escape, de-escalate, assert, or fight back.

CFA also teaches students to assess a variety of other important factors, including the assailant's demeanor, intent, range, positioning and weapon capability, as well as such environmental issues as escape routes, barriers, terrain, and makeshift weaponry. In addition to assessment skills, CFA also teaches students how to enhance perception and observation skills.

Analysis and Integration Skills

The analytical process is intricately linked to understanding how to defend yourself in any threatening situation. If you want to be the best, every aspect of fighting and personal protection must be dissected. Every strategy, tactic, movement, and concept must be broken down to its atomic parts. The three planes (physical, mental, spiritual) of self-defense must be unified scientifically through arduous practice and constant exploration.

CFA's most advanced practitioners have sound insight and understanding of a wide range of sciences and disciplines. They include human anatomy, kinesiology, criminal justice, sociology, kinesics, proxemics, combat physics, emergency medicine, crisis management, histrionics, police and military science, the psychology of aggression, and the role of archetypes.

Analytical exercises are also a regular part of CFA training. For example, we conduct problem-solving sessions involving particular assailants attacking in defined environments. We move hypothetical attackers through various ranges to provide insight into tactical solutions. We scrutinize different methods of attack for their general utility in combat. We also discuss the legal ramifications of self-defense on a frequent basis.

In addition to problem-solving sessions, students are slowly exposed to concepts of integration and modification. Oral and written examinations are given to measure intellectual accomplishment. Unlike systems, CFA does not use colored belts or sashes to identify the student's level of proficiency.

Philosophy

Philosophical resolution is essential to a fighter's mental confidence and clarity. Anyone learning the art of war must find the ultimate answers to questions concerning the use of violence in defense of himself or others. To advance to the highest levels of combat awareness, you must find clear and lucid answers to such provocative questions as could you take the life of another, what are your fears, who are you, why are you interested in studying Contemporary Fighting Arts, why are you reading this book, and what is good and what is evil? If you haven't begun the quest to formulate these important questions and answers, then take a break. It's time to figure out just why you want to know the laws and rules of destruction.

Cognitive Combat Skills

Cognitive combat exercises are also important for improving one's fighting skills. CFA uses visualization and crisis rehearsal scenarios to improve general body mechanics, tools and techniques, and maneuvers, as well as tactic selection. Mental clarity, concentration, and emotional control are also developed to enhance one's ability to call upon the controlled killer instinct.

The Spiritual Component

There are many tough fighters out there. In fact, they reside in every town in every country. However, most are nothing more than vicious animals that lack self-mastery. And self-mastery is what separates the true warrior from the eternal novice.

I am not referring to religious precepts or beliefs when I speak of CFA's spiritual component. Unlike most martial arts, CFA does not merge religion into its spiritual aspect. Religion is a very personal and private matter and should never, be incorporated into any fighting system. CFA's spiritual component is not something that is taught or studied. Rather, it is that which transcends the physical and mental aspects of being and reality. There is a deeper part of each of us that is a

13

tremendous source of truth and accomplishment.

In CFA, the spiritual component is something that is slowly and progressively acquired. During the challenging quest of combat training, one begins to tap the higher qualities of human nature. Those elements of our being that inherently enable us to know right from wrong and good from evil. As we slowly develop this aspect of our total self, we begin to strengthen qualities profoundly important to the "truth." Such qualities are essential to your growth through the mastery of inner peace, the clarity of your "vision," and your recognition of universal truths.

One of the goals of my system is to promote virtue and moral responsibility in people who have extreme capacities for physical and mental destructiveness. The spiritual component of fighting is truly the most difficult aspect of personal growth. Yet, unlike the physical component, where the practitioner's abilities will be limited to some degree by genetics and other natural factors, the spiritual component of combat offers unlimited potential for growth and development. In the final analysis, CFA's spiritual component poses the greatest challenges for the student. It is an open-ended plane of unlimited advancement.

CHAPTER ONE
Anatomy of Destruction

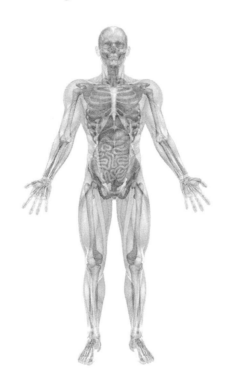

KNOWLEDGE IS POWER

Knowing how and when to strike the enemy is essential for street survival; however knowing *where* to hit him is equally important. Anyone who truly wants to neutralize a vicious criminal adversary in a self-defense crisis must have a working knowledge of the body targets on the human anatomy.

Contrary to popular belief, the human body has numerous structural weaknesses that are especially vulnerable to attack. The human body simply was not designed to withstand the punishment of strikes and blows. Always bear in mind that regardless of the attacker's size, strength, skill, or state of mind, he will always have vulnerable targets that can be exploited and attacked.

I'd be remiss if I didn't mention that every martial artist, self-defense practitioner, and combatives instructor has a moral and legal responsibility to know the medical implications of his offensive arsenal. The bottom line is, it's your responsibility to know which anatomical targets will stun, incapacitate, disfigure, cripple or kill your adversary. Not to mention, knowledge of the medical implications will make you a more efficient self-defense technician.

Unfortunately, there are some ignorant martial art and self-defense instructors who teach ineffective striking targets. For example, the biceps, collarbone, chest, kidneys, and coronal suture, are just a few targets that yield lousy results when struck. Such targets won't neutralize a vicious criminal immediately. In most cases, it will only piss him off and provoke him to attack you with greater viciousness and determination.

Therefore, it's essential to strike anatomical targets that will immediately incapacitate the enemy. Anything less can get you seriously injured or possibly killed.

The assailant's anatomical targets are located in one of three possible *target zones*. Zone One (head region) consists of targets related to the assailant's senses, including the eyes, temples, nose, chin, and back of neck. Zone Two (neck, torso, groin) consists of targets related to the assailant's breathing, including the throat, solar plexus, ribs, and groin. Zone Three (legs and feet) consists of anatomical targets related to the assailant's mobility, including the thighs, knees, shins, insteps, and toes. Now, lets take a good look at these targets and the medical implications of each.

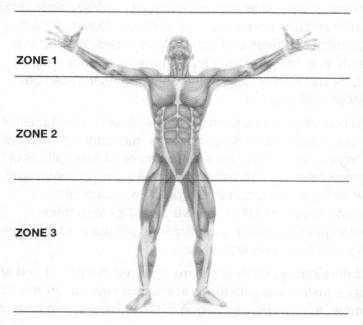

ZONE 1

ZONE 2

ZONE 3

EYES

Eyes sit in the orbital of the skull. They're ideal targets for street combat because they are one of the most important organs for your assailant to effectively fight. Not to mention that the eyes are extremely sensitive and difficult to protect. Also striking them requires minimal force.

The eyes can be poked, scratched, and gouged from a variety of angles and vantages. Depending on the force of your strike, it can cause numerous injuries, including watering of the eyes, hemorrhaging, blurred vision, temporary or permanent blindness, severe pain, rupture, shock, and even unconsciousness.

The assailant's probable reaction dynamic from a well targeted eye strike may include the following:

- He bends forward, shuts his eyes, screams from the pain.

- He covers his eyes with his hands.

- He freezes from shock.

EARS

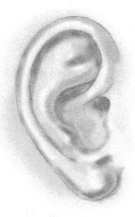

Like the eyes, the ears are extremely sensitive to attack. The opponent's ears can be punched, popped and torn. When struck with a moderate amount of force, the tympanic membrane (eardrum) will easily rupture.

Striking the ear can also result in percussive shock, extreme pain, unconsciousness, partial or complete loss of hearing, bleeding, disorientation, and loss of balance. You can use the following body weapons to attack the ears: cupped palm strike, punches, elbow strikes, fingers, and the knee strike.

The assailant's probable reaction dynamic from a well targeted ear strike may include the following:

- He bends forward, covers his ears.
- He collapses to the ground.
- He freezes from shock.

TEMPLE

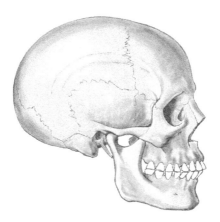

The temple or sphenoid bone is a thin, weak bone located on both sides of the skull approximately one inch from the assailant's eye. Because of its inherently weak structure and close proximity to the brain, a very powerful strike to this anatomical target can be deadly.

Other possible injuries include unconsciousness, hemorrhage, concussion, shock, and coma. You can use the following body weapons to strike the assailant's temple: elbow strikes, hook punches and in some cases the knee strike.

The opponent's probable reaction dynamic from a strike to the temple may include the following:

- His head and body fall sideways.
- His torso becomes exposed.
- His eyes shut from the impact.
- His arms and hands drop.
- He's knocked out cold.

NOSE

The nose is made up of a thin bone, cartilage, numerous blood vessels, and many nerves. It is a particularly good impact target because it stands out from the assailant's face and can be struck from three different directions (up, straight, down). A moderate blow can cause stunning pain, eye watering, temporary blindness, and hemorrhaging. A powerful strike can result in shock and unconsciousness. Lead straights, rear crosses, palm heels, upper cuts, hammer fists, elbow and knee strikes can be delivered effectively to the assailant's nose.

The opponent's probable reaction dynamic from a nose strike may include the following:

• He bends forward.

• He shuts his eyes.

• He covers his face with both his hands.

• He becomes temporarily immobilized.

• If temporary blindness occurs, he might grab hold of you.

CHIN

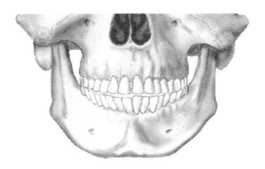

In western boxing, the chin is considered a *"knockout button"* responsible for retiring hundreds of boxers. It's also a great target for unarmed combat. When the chin is struck at a forty-five degree angle, shock waves are transmitted to the cerebellum and cerebral hemispheres of the brain, resulting in paralysis and immediate unconsciousness. Depending on the force of your blow, other possible injuries include broken jaw, concussion, and whiplash to the assailant's neck. Some of the best body weapons to strike the chin are: uppercuts, elbow strikes, knee strikes, palm heels and even head butts.

The opponent's probable reaction dynamic from a powerful chin strike may include the following:

- His head reels backward.
- His throat and torso become exposed.
- His centerline opens up.
- His arms and hands drop.
- He's knocked out cold.

BACK OF NECK

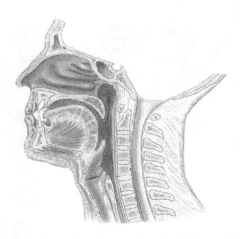

The back of the assailant's neck consists of the first seven vertebrae (also called the cervical vertebrae) of the spinal column. They function as a circuit board for nerve impulses from the brain to the body. The back of the neck is a lethal target because the vertebrae are poorly protected.

A very powerful strike to the back of the assailant's neck can cause shock, unconsciousness, a broken neck, complete paralysis, coma, and death. Two of the best body weapons to strike the cervical vertebra are hammer fists and elbow strikes.

The assailant's probable reaction dynamic from a powerful strike to the back of the neck may include the following:

- His head drops forward.
- His arms and hands drop.
- He's knocked out cold.

THROAT

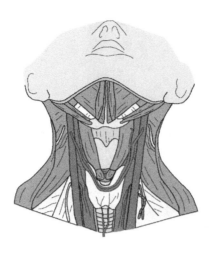

In a life and death self-defense situation, attacking your assailant's throat can save your life. The throat is considered a lethal target because a thin layer of skin only protects it. This region consists of the thyroid, hyaline, and crocoid cartilage, trachea, and larynx. The trachea, or windpipe, is a cartilaginous cylindrical tube that measures 4 ½ inches in length and approximately one inch in diameter.

A direct and powerful strike to this target may result in unconsciousness, blood drowning, massive hemorrhaging, air starvation, and death. If the thyroid cartilage is crushed, hemorrhaging will occur, the windpipe will quickly swell shut, and the assailant will die of suffocation.

The assailant's probable reaction dynamic from a throat strike may include the following:

- His head and body drop forward.
- He grabs or covers his throat with both hands.
- He struggles for air or goes into shock.
- He chokes and gags uncontrollably.

SOLAR PLEXUS

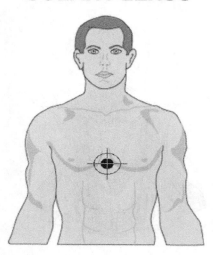

The solar plexus is a large collection of nerves situated below the sternum in the upper abdomen. A moderate blow to this area can cause nausea, pain, and shock, making it difficult for the adversary to properly breath. A powerful strike to the solar plexus can result in severe abdominal pain and cramping, air starvation, and shock.

The opponent's probable reaction dynamic from a strike to the solar plexus may include the following:

• He grabs and covers the center of his chest with one or both of his hands.

• He doubles over in pain.

• His body bends forward.

• He drops down on one knee.

• He struggles for air.

RIBS

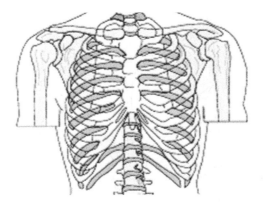

There is twelve pair of ribs in the human body. Excluding the eleventh and twelfth ribs, they are long and slender bones that are joined by the vertebral column in the back and the sternum and costal cartilage in the front. Since there are no eleventh and twelfth ribs (floating ribs) in the front, you should direct your strikes to the ninth and tenth ribs.

A moderate strike to the anterior region of the ribs may cause severe pain and shortness of breath. An extremely powerful forty-five degree blow could break the assailant's rib and force it into a lung, resulting in its collapse, internal hemorrhaging, air starvation, unconsciousness, excruciating pain, and possible death.

The opponent's probable reaction dynamic from a strike to the ribs may include the following:

• He grabs and covers the afflicted rib with either one or both of his hands.

   • He doubles over in pain.

   • His body bends forward.

   • He drops down on one knee.

   • He struggles for air.

27

GROIN

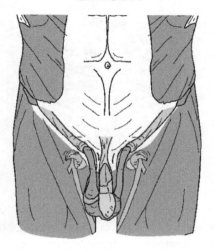

Every man will agree that the groin is an extremely sensitive target. The groin region (testes) can be kicked, stomped, punched or crushed. A moderate kick or strike to an assailant's groin can cause a variety of possible reaction: severe pain, nausea, vomiting, shortness of breath and possible sterility. A powerful strike to the groin may crush the scrotum and the testes against the pubic bones, causing shock and unconsciousness.

The assailant's probable reaction dynamic from a strike to the groin may include the following:

- His head and body violently drop forward.
- He grabs or covers his groin region.
- He struggles for breath.
- He momentarily freezes from shock.

THIGHS

Many fighters overlook the thighs as an impact target. In fact, because the thighs are a large and difficult to protect, they make excellent striking targets in a street fight.

While you can kick the thighs at a variety of different angles, the ideal location is the assailant's common peroneal nerve located on the side of the thigh, approximately four inches above the knee. Striking this area can result in extreme pain and immediate immobility of the afflicted leg. An extremely hard kick to the thigh may result in a fracture of the femur, internal bleeding, severe pain, intense cramping, and long-term immobility.

The opponent's probable reaction dynamic from a strike to the thigh may include the following:

- His afflicted leg buckles.
- His body weight shifts backwards.
- His body drops forward.
- His arms drop down to his sides.

KNEES

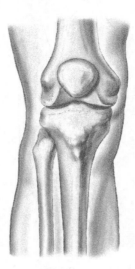

The knees are relatively weak joints that are held together by a number of supporting ligaments. When the assailant's leg is locked or fixed in position and a forceful strike is delivered to the front of the joint, the cruciate ligaments will tear, resulting in excruciating pain, swelling, and immobility.

Located on the front of the knee joint is the patella, which is made of a small, loose piece of bone. The patella is also vulnerable to possible dislocation by a direct, forceful kick. Severe pain, swelling, and immobility may also result.

The assailant's probable reaction dynamic from a knee strike may include the following:

- His afflicted leg locks in place.
- His body weight shifts backwards.
- His head and body drops forward.
- His arms drop down to his sides.

SHINS

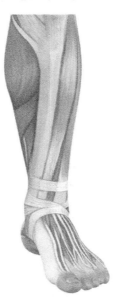

Everyone, at one time or another, has knocked his or her shin bone into the end of a table or bed accidentally and felt the intense pain associated with it. The shin is very sensitive because the bone is only protected by a thin layer of skin. However, a powerful kick delivered to this target can easily fracture it, resulting in nauseating pain, hemorrhaging, and immobility.

The opponent's probable reaction dynamic from a shin kick may include the following:

- His afflicted leg locks in place.
- His body weight shifts backwards.
- His body drops forward.
- His arms drop down to his sides.

TOES/INSTEP

With a powerful stomp of your heel, you can break the small bones of an assailant's toes and or instep, causing severe pain and immobility. Stomping on the toes is an excellent technique for releasing many holds. It should be mentioned, however, that you should avoid an attack to the toes/instep if the attacker is wearing hard leather boots, i.e., combat, hiking, or motorcycle boots.

The opponent's probable reaction dynamic from a shin kick may include the following:

- He'll raise his afflicted leg off the ground.
- His attention will shift to the ground.
- He'll be unable to walk or support his bodyweight.

HANDS/FINGERS

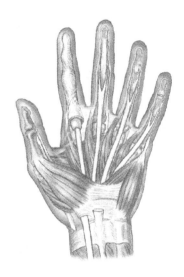

The hands and fingers are considered weak and vulnerable targets that can easily be jammed, sprained, broken, torn, and bitten. While a broken finger might not stop an attacker, it will certainly make him release his hold. A broken finger also makes it difficult for the assailant to clench his fist or hold a weapon. When attempting to break an assailant's finger, it's best to grab the pinkie and forcefully tear backward against the knuckle.

The probable reaction dynamic from a hand or finger injury may include:

- He instinctively retracts his hand into his body.
- He covers/protects his afflicted hand with his other hand.
- He's incapable of clenching his fist.
- He's unable to maintain a grip on his weapon.
- If he's holding or grabbing you, he'll release his grip.

Here's a list of ineffectual anatomical targets that will yield poor results in unarmed combat. NOTE: This list doesn't apply to armed combat (i.e., firearms, knives, edged weapons, etc).

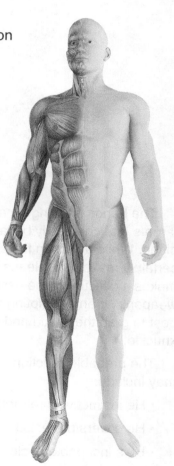

- Coronal Suture (the two frontal and parietal bones)
- Mastoid
- Sternocleidomastoid region
- Brachial Plexus
- Trapezius muscle
- Spleen
- Kidneys
- Bladder
- Biceps
- Elbow
- Radial nerve
- Heart
- Abdominal muscles
- Coccyx
- Gastrocnemius muscle
- Achilles tendon

CHAPTER TWO
Warrior's Cache

NATURAL BODY WEAPONS

The War Machine has a complete working knowledge of his natural body weapons. Body weapons are specific body parts that can be used to disable, cripple or kill a criminal assailant. Keep in mind that the lethality of a natural body weapon is predicated on two critical factors: the target that you select and the amount of force you deliver. Natural body weapons include the head, teeth, voice, elbows, fists, heel of palm, fingers, web of hand, edge of hand, knees, shins, dorsum of foot, heel of foot and ball of foot. Lets take a look at each one is greater detail.

THE HEAD

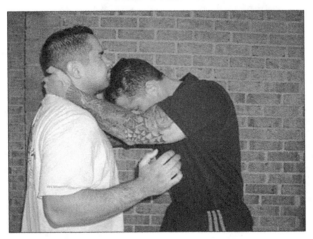

In close quarter combat, the War Machine uses his head for butting the assailant. Head butts are also ideal when your attacker has placed you in a hold where your arms are pinned against your sides.

There are two types of head butts: clipping and ramming. The clipping head butt is executed in a downward direction to the opponent's nose while the ramming head butt is generally directed upwards against a taller foe. The head butt can also be delivered in four different directions: (1) Forward; (2) Backward; (3) Right Side; (4) Left Side.

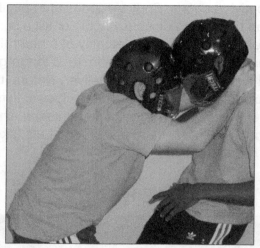

Here, students practice full-contact head butts with head gear.

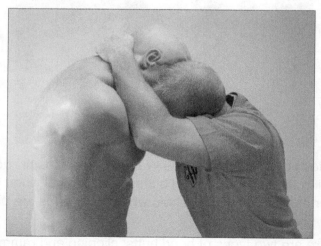

If a training partner isn't available, you can safely practice the head butt on the body opponent bag.

THE TEETH

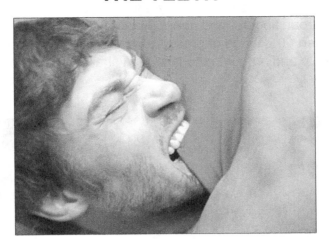

When engaged in grappling range, your teeth can be used for biting anything on the assailant's body (i.e. nose, ears, throat, fingers, biceps, etc.). When biting it's important to penetrate deep and hard with your molars and shake your head vigorously back and forth.

While a deep penetrating bite is extremely painful, it also transmits a powerful psychological message to your assailant. It lets him know that you mean business and are willing to do anything to survive the encounter. This is especially helpful for smaller men and women who don't have the physical size and strength to defend against large and powerful criminal attackers.

CAUTION: Biting should only be used as a last resort; you run the risk of contracting communicable diseases.

When ground fighting, the teeth can be used to bite anywhere on the enemy's body. Ideal targets include the nose, ears, throat, fingers, and arms. Since the average person can only exert 60 pounds of pressure when biting, it's important to bite deep and hard into the flesh and shake your head vigorously.

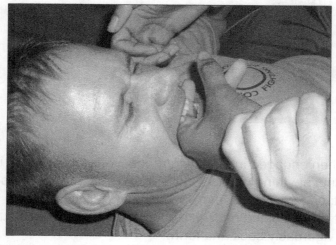

Despite how powerful your adversary might be, his fingers will always be his weakest link.

WARNING: Biting the opponent's flesh will permanently disfigure him, so be absolutely certain your actions are legally and morally justified in the eyes of the law.

THE VOICE

The voice can be a powerful weapon. When fighting, the yell is a natural manifestation of the voice. The yell was probably part of earliest man's expressions. He undoubtedly used the yell in his life-and-death battles long before he learned the most basic forms of spoken language. The North American Indians were proficient in using the yell to strike fear in their enemies.

Yelling actually serves a strategic purpose in self-defense. Yelling in combat can distract, startle, and temporarily paralyze your assailant. It can cause him to freeze in his tracks, allowing you that split second advantage to deliver the first debilitating strike and thus to gain offensive control.

Yelling can also be used to psyche out the adversary. Imagine this situation: one minute you're talking calmly to a threatening aggressor and the next you are suddenly emitting a blood-curdling yell and striking him. This dramatic reversal can throw an assailant into a psychological tailspin.

Yelling also synchronizes your state of mind with the physical process taking place. It is the catalyst that sets off the killer instinct. It is the primal expression that harbors the killer instinct. In addition, yelling actually may draw attention to your emergency situation. In many cases, muggers, rapists, and street punks will abort their attacks and run to avoid detection.

A good place to practice yelling is in your car. The interior of the car insulates and amplifies your voice, giving you a good sense of its effectiveness. Practice prolonged yells and intermittent, explosive ones. The yell should also be used judiciously in sparring and simulated combat scenarios to test its shock value.

41

THE ELBOWS

Elbows strikes are devastating weapons that can be used in the grappling range. They are explosive, deceptive, and very difficult to stop. Elbows can generally be delivered horizontally, vertically, and diagonally. Targets include the assailant's temple, throat, chin, cervical vertebrae, ribs, and solar plexus. When delivering elbow strikes, be certain to pivot your hips and shoulder forcefully in the direction of your blow.

Vertical Elbow - The vertical elbow strike travels vertically to the assailant's face, throat, or body. It can be executed from either the right or left side of the body. To perform the strike, raise your elbow vertically (with the elbow flexed) until your hand is next to the side of your head. The striking surface is the point of the elbow. The power for this strike is acquired through the quick extension of the legs at the moment of impact.

Horizontal Elbow - The horizontal elbow strike travels horizontally to the assailant's face, throat, or body. It can also be executed from either the right or left side of the body. To perform the strike, begin from the on-guard hand position, then rotate your hips and shoulders horizontally into your target.

Your palms should be facing downward with your hand next to the side of your head. The striking surface is the elbow point.

Diagonal Elbow (traveling downward) - The diagonal elbow strike travels diagonally downward to the assailant's face, throat, or body. It can be delivered from either the right or left side of the body. To execute the strike, rotate your elbow back, up, and over while quickly whipping it downward to your desired target. Bend your knees as your body descends with the strike. Your palm should be facing away from when making contact. The striking surface is the elbow point.

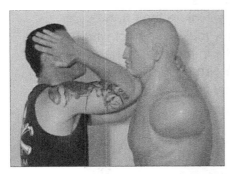

Pictured left, Franco demonstrates a vertical elbow strike on the body opponent bag.

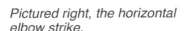

Pictured right, the horizontal elbow strike.

Pictured left, Franco delivers a diagonal elbow strike.

43

THE FISTS

The fists are specifically used for punching the enemy's nose, temple, chin, throat, solar plexus, ribs, and in some cases, groin. Punching is a true art form that requires considerable training and practice to master. Moreover, I strongly recommend that women avoid punching with their fists altogether. Females generally have small hands, weak wrists and long nails, all of which will lead to broken hands, wrists and fingers!

Some self-defense practitioners are reluctant to employ fisted blows for fear that they will injure their hands. Be forewarned! When a fisted blow makes contact with the opponent's skull, it often results in a fractured hand. While it's true that open hand blows are generally safer to deliver than fisted strikes, both are essential for street combat.

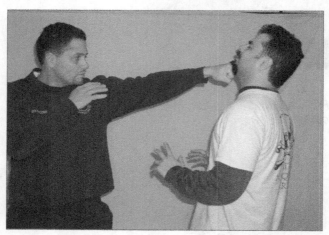

Here, the author (left) demonstrates a lead straight. The lead straight is a linear punch thrown from your lead arm and contact is made with the center knuckle.

To execute this blow, quickly twist your lead leg, hip, and shoulder forward. Snap your blow into the assailant's target and return back to the starting position. A common mistake is to throw the punch and let it deflect off to the side. Targets for the lead straight include: nose, chin, and solar plexus.

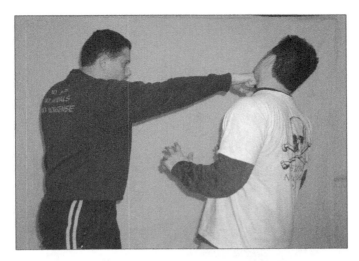

In this photograph, Franco launches a rear cross. The rear cross is the most powerful linear tool in your unarmed arsenal. This punch travels in a straight direction to your assailant's nose, chin or solar plexus. Proper waist twisting and weight transfer is of paramount importance to the rear cross. You must shift your weight from your rear foot to your lead leg as you throw the punch. Torquing your rear foot, hip and shoulder into the direction of the blow can generate bone-crushing force.

To maximize the impact of the punch, make certain that your fist is positioned horizontally. Avoid overextending the blow or exposing your chin during its execution.

Punching effectively is truly an art form, requiring considerable time and training to master. When punching, hit with your center knuckle. This will maximize the impact of your blow, afford proper skeletal alignment, and prevent wrist sprains.

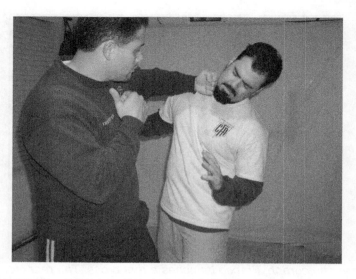

The hook punch is one of the most devastating blows in your arsenal. However, it's also one of the most difficult to master. To properly execute the hook punch, you must maintain the proper wrist, forearm, and shoulder alignment. When delivering the strike, be certain your arm is bent at least ninety degrees and that your wrist and forearm are kept straight throughout the movement.

To execute the hook punch, quickly and smoothly, raise your elbow up so that your arm is parallel to the ground when torquing your shoulder, hip, and foot into the direction of the blow. As you throw the punch, make certain that your fist is positioned vertically.

WARNING: Never position your fist horizontally when throwing a hook. This inferior hand placement can cause a sprained or broken wrist.

The shovel hook is a powerful punch that travels diagonally into your assailant. Like the hook punch, this blow can be delivered from both the lead and rear sides. Here is a good way to remember the proper angle of this punch: if the hook punch is positioned at three o'clock and your uppercut is at six o'clock, then your shovel hook is positioned between three and six o'clock.

To properly execute the rear shovel hook, dip your shoulder and simultaneously twist your rear leg and hip into your target and then drive your entire body into the assailant. Once again, keep balanced and follow through your selected target.

When delivering a blow from a stationary position, apply the "stabilizer and mover" theory. This means torquing one side of your body (the striking side) while simultaneously stabilizing the other side. Applying this theory of body mechanics maximizes the power of your blows and minimizes your loss of balance.

47

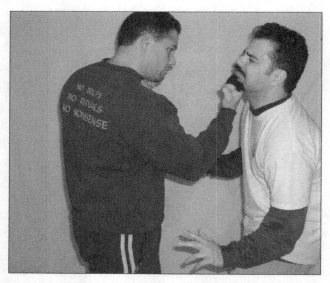

The uppercut is a powerful blow that can be delivered in both the punching and grappling ranges. This fractal tool travels in a vertical direction to either the assailant's chin or body, and it can be delivered from either the lead or rear arm.

To execute the uppercut, quickly twist and lift your body in the direction of the blow. Make certain that the punch has a short arc and that you avoid any "winding up" motions.

The uppercut is considered a fractal technique that can be deployed in both the punching and grappling ranges of unarmed combat.

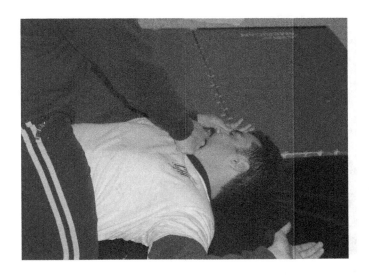

Punching skills also play a vital role when ground fighting. For example, the pummel tactic is generally applied when you have mounted your assailant and your hands are free to strike. Once your balance is established in the mounted position, proceed with a vicious furry of offensive strikes designed to take your assailant out of the fight. The power of your blows are not such a critical concern because you have the gravitational advantage and your assailant's head is flush against the floor (the ground functions as a stabilizer that concentrates your impact).

The best blows for the pummel assault are the following: tight linear punches, tight hooks, hammer fists, and in some cases elbow strikes.

WARNING: Because of the vicious characteristics of the pummel tactic, spectator intervention is a strong possibility. Be aware of your surroundings at all times!

The grappling dummy is an excellent piece of equipment for developing the pummeling technique. Here, a student throws a series of linear punches.

Remember, pummeling your assailant from the mounted position can be deadly and must always be legally and morally justified in the eyes of the law!

THE PALMS

The palm heel strike is a powerful open-hand linear blow that can be delivered from both the lead and rear arm. Contact is made with the heel of your palm with the fingers pointing up. Targets include your assailant's nose and chin.

When delivering the blow, be certain to torque your shoulder, hips and foot into the direction of the strike. Make certain that your arm extends straight and the heel of your palm makes contact with either the assailant's nose or chin. Return to the starting position. Remember to retract your arm in the same line that you initiated it.

The chin is the ideal target for the palm heel. Striking the chin transmits shock to the cerebellum and cerebral hemispheres of the brain, resulting in paralysis and immediate unconsciousness. Other possible injuries include broken jaw, concussion and whiplash.

As demonstrated in our Widowmaker Program, the palms can also be used for Webbing the adversary. CFA's Webbing strike is a multi-purpose fighting technique that can be applied in a variety of combat situations.

THE FINGERS

The fingers are used for jabbing, gouging, and clawing the eyes, and pulling, tearing, and crushing the throat and testicles. Strong fingers and hands are important to the War Machine. They improve tearing, crushing and gouging techniques as well as overall clinching skills. In addition, knife-disarming techniques are safer and weapon retention techniques are more effective. Strong fingers and hands also tend to improve the structural integrity of fisted blows.

A very effective way to strengthen your hands, wrists and forearms is to work out with heavy duty hand grippers. While there are many on the market, I prefer the Captains of Crush brand. These high quality grippers are virtually indestructible and they are sold in a variety of different resistance levels ranging from 60 to 365 pounds.

53

The finger jab is a quick, non telegraphic strike executed from your lead arm. Contact is made with your fingertips. The strike is likened to that of a snakebite. To execute the finger jab properly, quickly shoot your arm out and back. Don't tense your muscles prior to the execution of the strike. Just relax and send it out.

Targets for the finger jab are the assailant's eyes. Don't forget that a finger jab strike can cause temporary or permanent blindness, severe pain, and shock. With the finger jab, you want speed, accuracy, and, above all, non telegraphic movement.

The double-thumb gouge is a nuclear grappling tactic that can produce devastating results. This tactic can be delivered when either standing or fighting on the ground. To perform the gouge, place one hand on each side of the assailant's face. Stabilize your hands by wrapping your fingers around both sides of your assailant's jaw. Immediately drive both your thumbs into the assailant's eye sockets. Maintain and increase forceful pressure. The double-thumb gouge can cause temporary or permanent blindness, shock, and unconsciousness. WARNING: The double-thumb gouge should only be used in life-and-death situations! Be certain that it is legally warranted and justified.

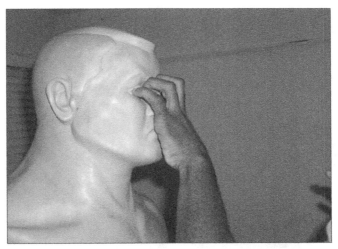

Clawing and raking the criminal's eyes are very effective in the clinch range. The eyes are extremely sensitive, very difficult to protect, and injuring them requires very little force. The eyes can be clawed from a variety of angles. Attacking this target can result in watering of the eyes, hemorrhaging, blurred vision, temporary or permanent blindness, extreme pain, rupture and shock.

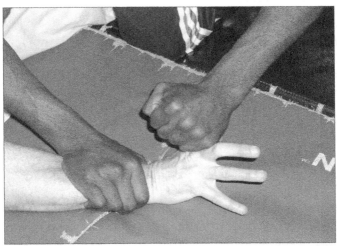

Ironically, your fingers can also attack the opponent's fingers. One of the best strategies when fighting a seasoned grappler is to break his fingers.

Strong fingers will allow you to crush the enemy's throat. Crushing techniques can be employed when standing in grappling range or lying in the prone position. The two primary crushing targets are the assailant's throat and testicles. Crushing the assailant's throat is not an easy task. It requires quick and exact digit placement, sufficient leverage accompanied with the vicious determination to destroy your assailant.

WARNING: Throat attacks should only be used in life and death situations. Never attack the throat unless it is legally and morally justified in the eyes of the law. Here, Sammy Franco attacks his adversary with extreme prejudice!

If you want devastating crushing power, you'll need to condition your wrists and forearms by performing various forearm exercises with free weights. Exercises like hammer curls, reverse curls, wrist curls are great for developing powerful forearms.

WEB OF HAND

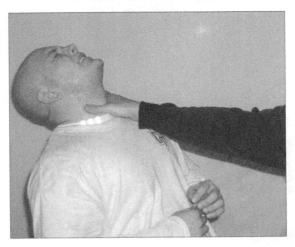

The web of the hand is specifically used to attack the assailant's throat. The throat is a lethal target because it's only protected by a thin layer of skin. This target region consists of the thyroid, hyaline and crocoid cartilage, trachea, and larynx. The trachea, or windpipe, is a cartilaginous cylindrical tube that measures 4 1/2 inches in length and is approximately 1 inch in diameter. A powerful web hand strike to the throat can easily result in unconsciousness, blood drowning, massive hemorrhaging, air starvation, and death. WARNING! Always be certain your actions are legally and morally justified in the eyes of the law!

WARNING! Attacking the throat can be deadly! Always be certain your actions are legally and morally justified in the eyes of the law!

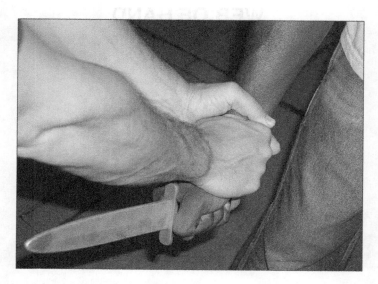

The web of the hand also plays a vital role when defending against a knife attack. The V-grip is applied by grabbing the assailant's wrist with both of your hands (make certain that the webs of your hands completely envelop your assailant's wrist.) Once you have made contact, squeeze hard and hold on with all your might. When applied correctly, the V-grip will allow you to forcefully pull and redirect the knife away from your body targets.

Once you've gained solid control over your attacker's knife hand using the V-grip, it's critical to attack him as viciously as possible. Drive your knee repeatedly into his groin, stomp on his instep, head-butt his nose, and bite into his jugular if necessary. Attack him repeatedly with cold determination. Your life is on the line!

EDGE OF HAND

With little training, you can throw the edge of your hand in a whip like motion to surprise and neutralize your attacker. By whipping your arm horizontally to his throat, you can cause severe injury or death.

The knife hand strike is another tool that can be delivered in both grappling and punching ranges. It can be delivered from both the lead and rear sides, and it can also be delivered from a variety of possible angles: (1) Horizontally; (2) Vertically; (3) Diagonally.

To properly deliver the horizontal knife hand, quickly whip the edge of your hand into the assailant's throat. Make certain to follow-through the target.

 *The knife hand strike is best used during multiple attacker situations when your attackers have flanked you inside of punching range.*

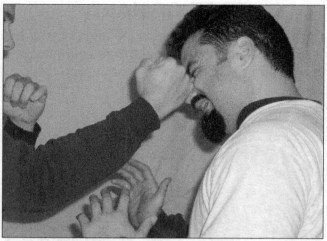

The short arc hammer fist is a quick and powerful strike delivered at close range. Your target is the opponent's nose. To deliver this strike, begin by raising your fist with your elbow flexed. Quickly whip your clenched fist down in a vertical line onto the bridge of the assailant's nose. Remember to keep your elbow bent on impact and maintain your balance.

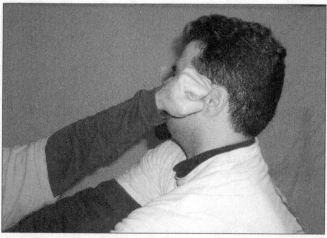

The horizontal hammer fist is another powerful strike that is delivered horizontally to the assailant's chin or temple. To deliver this strike, simultaneously torque your shoulder and hip into the direction of the blow. Keep your elbow slightly bent on impact and maintain your balance.

THE KNEES

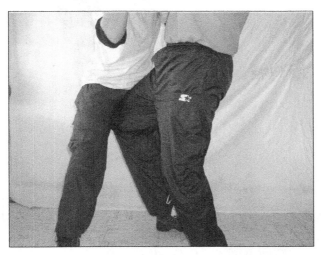

The knee strike is another devastating close-quarter grappling range tool that can instantly bring a formidable assailant down to the ground. The knee strike can be delivered vertically and diagonally to a variety of anatomical targets including: common peroneal nerve, quadriceps, groin, ribs, and in some cases the face. When delivering the knee strike, make certain to make contact with your patella and not your lower thigh. To guarantee sufficient power, deliver all your knee strikes with your rear leg.

When delivering the vertical knee strike, keep your rear leg bent with your toes pointed to the ground. This toe position provides the following: (1) helps maintain proper skeletal alignment, (2) promotes muscular relaxation, (3) protects your toes from unnecessary injury, and (4) facilitates rapid delivery.

The rear diagonal knee strike travels on a diagonal plane to the assailant's common peroneal nerve, quadriceps, groin, ribs, and in some cases the face. When delivering the strike, don't forget to follow through your target.

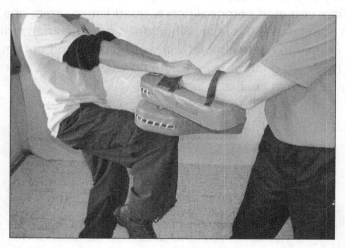

Oversized focus mitts are ideal for developing explosive knee strikes. Be certain to keep the mitts clear of your body!

Knee strikes can be particularly effective when ground fighting. In this photo, a student drives a vertical knee into his opponent's groin.

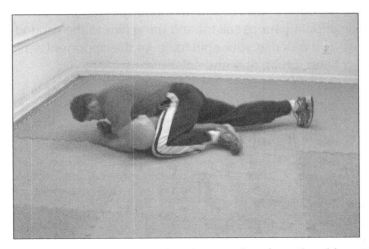

Pictured here, a student practices knee strikes from the side mount position. Warning! Knee strikes to the head can be deadly!

THE SHINS

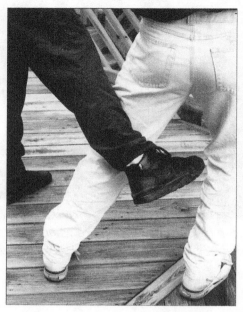

The shinbone is a very powerful body weapon that can quickly cripple your assailant and bring him to the ground in agony. You can use your shin to strike the opponent's thigh, side of knee, groin, ribs and solar plexus.

Pictured here, Franco works the hook kick on the cylindrical bag. Notice how contact is made with his shin bone.

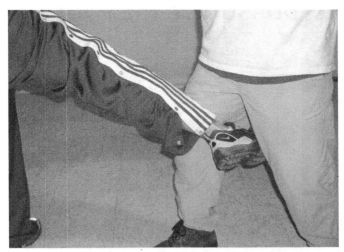

The hook kick is thrown from your rear leg. Contact is made with either your instep or shinbone. It's, by far, the most powerful kick you can deliver, because you are torquing your entire body into the target.

To execute the hook kick, step at a 45-degree angle and simultaneously twist and drive your rear leg and hip into your target. Make certain to pivot your base foot and follow through your target.

When executing the hook kick, either aim for your assailant's knee or drive your shin into the assailant's common peroneal nerve (approximately 4 inches above the knee). This will collapse and temporarily immobilize the assailant's leg. Keep in mind that if you strike the knee you can cause permanent damage to the cartilage, ligaments, and tendons.

When executing a hook kick, always allow your kick to sink into your assailant's leg briefly. This will maximize the force and penetration of your kick.

65

DORSUM OF THE FOOT

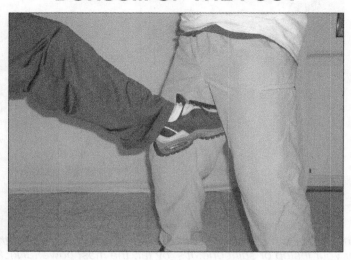

You can use the dorsum of the foot to execute a vertical kick to the assailant's groin, ribs and, in some cases, his face. Striking with the dorsum of the foot (shoe lace area) increases the power of your kick, prevents broken or jammed toes and also lengthens the surface area of your strike.

The Vertical kick can be delivered in three different directions - vertically, at a right angle, and at a left angle.

The vertical kick is one of the fastest kicks used in combat. This kick is delivered off your lead leg and travels on a vertical path to the assailant's groin and, in some cases, his face. To execute this kick, maintain your balance while quickly shifting your weight back to your rear leg and simultaneously raising your lead leg vertically into the assailant's groin. Once contact is made, quickly force your leg back to the ground. Keep your supporting leg bent for balance.

When delivering a vertical kick, be certain to make contact with your instep. The instep is a good impact tool because it increases the power of your kick, prevents broken toes, and also lengthens the surface area of your natural body weapon.

When performing the vertical kick, avoid the tendency to snap your knee as you deliver the kick. Let your hip flexor muscle do all the work instead.

As a strict rule of thumb, always keep your hands up when performing the vertical kick.

The dorsum of your foot is extremely strong and can deliver a devastating kick. In this photo, a vertical kick is delivered to the knife attacker's chin. This technique is called "punting" and it is only permitted in self-defense situations that warrant the use of deadly force.

BALL OF THE FOOT

You can use the ball of your foot to execute a push kick into the assailant's thigh. You can also snap it quickly into the assailant's shin to loosen a grab from the front. When striking the assailants with the ball of your foot, be certain to pull your toes back to avoid jamming or breaking them.

A successful push kick frequently causes the adversary to reflexively drop his hand guard down, allowing you to move in and exploit target opportunities.

The push kick is another efficient kick delivered from your lead leg. To deliver the kick, quickly shift your weight to your rear leg and simultaneously raise your lead leg. Thrust the ball of your foot into the assailant's groin, quadriceps, knee, or shin. Quickly drop your leg to the ground. Make certain to keep your supporting leg bent for balance.

When delivering a push kick into the assailant's quadriceps, it's very important to make contact with the ball of your foot. This action will maximize the penetration of the kick into the assailant's muscle and nerves. You can also quickly snap the ball of the foot into the assailant's shinbone to loosen front grabs.

When kicking the assailant with the ball of your foot, remember to pull your toes back to avoid jamming or breaking them.

70

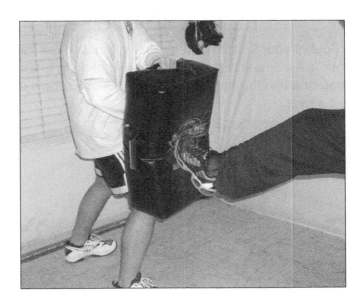

The striking shield is a versatile piece of training equipment that develops power in most of your kicks, punches, and strikes. This rectangular-shaped shield is constructed of foam and vinyl and is designed to withstand tremendous punishment.

As with focus mitt training, your partner plays a vital role in a good striking shield workout. He must hold the shield at the proper height and angle while simultaneously moving in and out of the ranges of combat. The intensity of your workout will depend on his ability to push you to your limit. Pictured here, the push kick in action.

When using the kicking shield, your training partner must learn how to absorb powerful kicks without losing his balance or injuring himself. Remember to start off slowly and build up the intensity.

71

HEEL OF THE FOOT

The heel of your foot is used for delivering sidekicks to the assailant's knee or shinbone. Also, when fighting in grappling range, you can use the heel of your foot to stomp down on the opponent's toes.

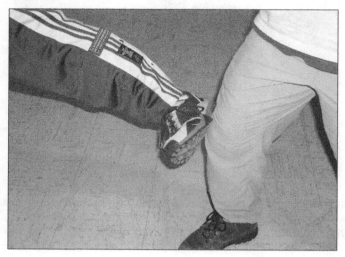

Pictured here, the side kick.

The side kick is a powerful linear kick executed from the lead leg. Contact is made with the heel. To execute the kick, shift your weight back, pivot your rear foot, and simultaneously raise and thrust your lead hip and leg into the assailant.

Remember that you must pivot your rear foot to facilitate proper skeletal alignment (shoulder, hip, and heel alignment). The side kick is targeted for either the assailant's hip, thigh, knee, or shinbone.

One important considerations when executing a sidekick is maintaining proper skeletal alignment. Skeletal alignment is the proper alignment or arrangement of your body, which maximizes the structural integrity of your kick. Therefore, when executing this kick always make certain that your heel, knee, hip, and shoulder align together.

73

The foot stomp is a deceptive close-quarter grappling strike that can break the small bones of the assailant's toes, causing severe pain and immediate immobility. Stomping on the assailant's toes is also one of the best ways for releasing many holds.

Keep in mind that you should avoid attacking the toes if the attacker is wearing hard leather boots, (i.e., combat, hiking or motorcycle boots).

To perform the foot stomp, raise your lead foot approximately ten inches from the ground and forcibly stomp on the assailant's toes with the heel of your foot.

If you doubt the effectiveness of a foot stomp, consider this sobering fact: a woman wearing high heel shoes can generate up to 1,600 pounds of pressure per square inch when delivering the foot stomp. Ouch!

CHAPTER THREE
Engage The Enemy

A DEFENSIVE CONUNDRUM

Defense it is a fundamental concept found in every martial art. In some systems it's a foundational philosophy; in others it's a strategic approach to combat. For example, most self-defense instructors, both traditional and modern, stress defensive responses rather than offensive action in a violent street encounter. It's also interesting that most katas (forms) begin and end with a block, illustrating a defensive attitude of most Karate systems. Defense is, without a doubt, the staple of most conventional martial art systems and styles.

Unfortunately, defensive approaches to real life combat can be disastrous. The self-defense technician who approaches combat defensively runs the risk of severe injury or even death. Allowing the criminal assailant the first offensive move is absolutely insane; it's like allowing a gunslinger the first draw. Never forget that the fighter who initiates usually wins most violent confrontations. It's that simple, folks.

Unlike conventional martial arts, the War Machine combat methodology is predicated on offense. Therefore, if combat is unavoidable, he takes the initiative and strikes first, fast, and with authority. You must accept this offensive philosophy and master the *compound attack* if you are to prevail in a vicious street fight.

THE COMPOUND ATTACK

A *compound attack* is the logical sequence of two or more tools launched in succession. The warrior gains the upper hand by initiating a flurry of full force, full speed strikes designed to overwhelm the opponent's defenses. The ultimate objective is to take the fight out of the adversary and the adversary out of the fight.

Based on power, directness, speed, and commitment, the compound attack also requires calculation, control, and clarity.

In other words, the unskilled, untrained brute that goes off with a buzz saw of violent strikes is not executing a compound attack. There is more to it than that I assure you.

The compound attack starts with a thorough knowledge of every conceivable target presented by the various stances and movements of the opponent. Unless your adversary is in full body armor, there are always targets. It's a question of recognizing them and striking quickly with the appropriate tools. This requires mastery of a wide range of offensive tools, knowledge of probable reaction dynamics and a complete understanding of ranges of unarmed combat.

But remember, what is universally true of the opponent is equally true of you. If there is the target available on him, there's always one on you, although vulnerability can be reduced with proper training. Thus the cardinal rule of the War Machine: strike first, strike fast, strike with authority and keep the pressure on.

As you attack one target, others open up naturally. It's up to you to recognize the opponent's reaction dynamics and maintain the offensive flow. Executed properly, the compound attack demolishes your opponents' defenses so that you ultimately take him down and out. It sounds great, but you must realize that it has to happen literally within seconds.

You cannot train enough in the compound method of attack. The warrior must always focus on power and relentless directness. In Contemporary Fighting Arts, we believe that true offense rests in the compound attack. It is efficient, effective, direct and destructive. When the chips are down, it's your only sure chance of survival.

Now that you're familiar with the structural weaknesses of various anatomical targets (Chapter One) and you have a sound understanding of the natural body weapons (Chapter two), it's time to put everything into action.

What follows are twenty different compound attack

scenarios. Since each and every fight is unique, these scenarios only serve as examples of possible combinations that can be deployed in combat.

COMPOUND ATTACK #1
(Vertical Kick-Rear Uppercut-Knee Strike)

1. Franco (right) assumes a de-escalation stance.

2. Franco launches a vertical kick to the opponent's groin.

79

3. He follows up with a rear uppercut to the chin.

4. Franco completes his attack with a vertical knee strike.

COMPOUND ATTACK #2
(Rear Palm Heel-Lead Hook Punch-Rear Hook Punch-Rear Vertical Knee)

1. Franco (right) assumes a de-escalation stance.

2. Franco attacks first with a rear palm heel strike.

81

3. He follows up with a lead hook punch.

4. Followed by a rear hook punch.

5. The adversary is finished off with a rear vertical knee strike.

COMPOUND ATTACK #3
(Rear Vertical Elbow-Lead Horizontal Elbow-Rear Horizontal Elbow-Diagonal Knee)

1. Franco (right) assumes a de-escalation stance.

2. Franco delivers a quick vertical elbow to the opponent's chin.

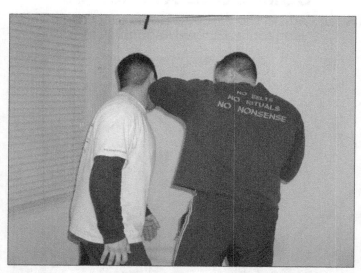

3. Franco exploits his opponent's reaction dynamics with a lead horizontal elbow.

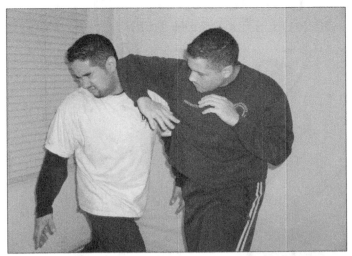

4. He follows up with a rear horizontal elbow strike.

5. The compound attack is complete with a rear diagonal knee.

COMPOUND ATTACK #4
(Push Kick-Uppercut-Double Thumb Gouge-Head Butt)

1. The adversary threatens Franco in kicking range.

2. Franco launches a push kick to the opponent's thigh.

3. He follows up with a rear uppercut to the chin.

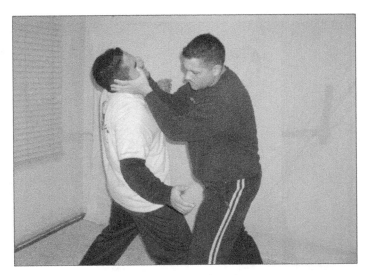

4. Next, a double thumb gouge.

87

5. A clipping head butt completes the compound attack.

COMPOUND ATTACK #5
(Finger Jab-Palm Heel-Head Butt-Diagonal Knee)

1. The trouble starts in punching range.

2. Franco's first strike is a quick finger jab to the eyes.

3. Followed by a rear pam heel strike.

4. Franco engages the clinch and delivers a head butt.

5. He completes his attack with a rear diagonal knee strike.

COMPOUND ATTACK #6

(Web Hand-Double Thumb Gouge-Head Butt-Vertical Knee)

1. Franco (right) assumes a first strike stance.

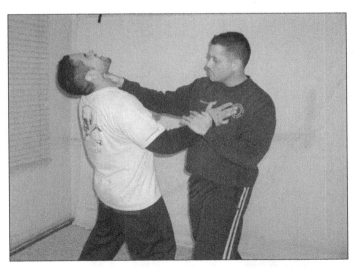

2. He attacks with a rear web hand strike to the assailant's throat.

3. Next, a double thumb gouge.

4. While maintaining the clinch, Franco delivers a head butt.

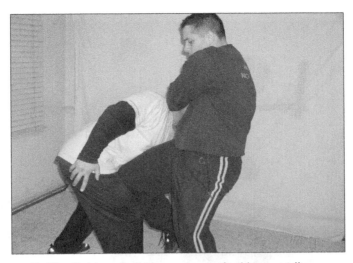

5. The fight ends with a rear vertical knee strike.

COMPOUND ATTACK #7
(Short Arc Hammer Fist-Hook Punch-Uppercut-Vertical Knee)

1. The adversary encroaches upon Franco.

93

2. Franco launches a hammer fist to the opponent's nose.

3. He follows up with a lead hook punch.

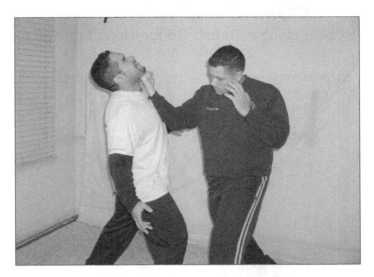

4. Next is the rear uppercut to the chin.

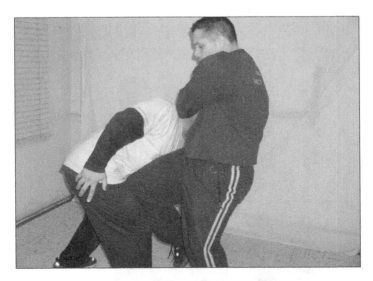

5. The fight ends with a rear vertical knee strike.

COMPOUND ATTACK #8
(Webbing-Double Thumb Gouge-Head Butt-Diagonal Knee Strike)

1. Franco (right) assumes a first strike stance.

2. He executes a Webbing strike to the chin.

3. Franco closes in with a double thumb gouge.

4. Followed by a head butt.

5. He completes his attack with a diagonal knee strike to the thigh.

COMPOUND ATTACK #9

(Short Arc Hammer Fist-Double Thumb Gouge-Knee Strike)

1. The adversary encroaches upon Franco.

2. Franco launches a hammer fist to the opponent's nose.

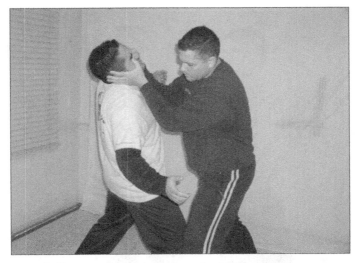

3. Franco closes in with a double thumb gouge.

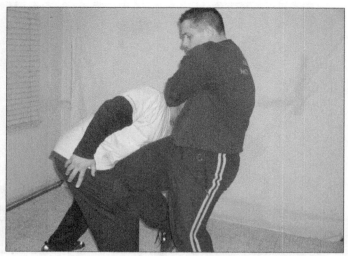

4. The fight ends with a rear vertical knee strike.

COMPOUND ATTACK #10
(Finger Jab-Uppercut-Lead Horizontal Elbow-Rear
Horizontal Elbow)

1. The adversary encroaches upon Franco.

2. Franco launches a finger jab to the opponent's eyes.

3. He follows up with a rear uppercut to the chin.

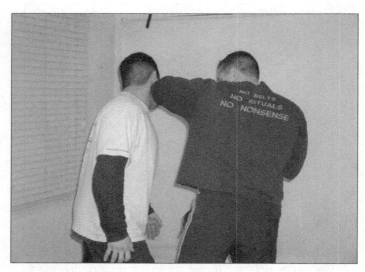

4. Franco exploits his opponent's reaction dynamics with a lead horizontal elbow.

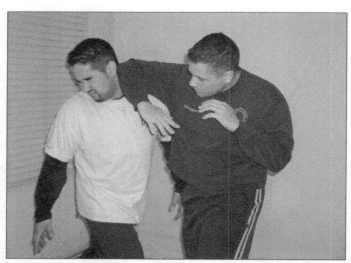

5. The compound attack is complete with a rear horizontal elbow.

COMPOUND ATTACK #11
(Palm Heel-Eye Rake-Lead Horizontal Elbow-Rear Horizontal Elbow)

1. Franco (right) assumes a de-escalation stance.

2. He begins his attack with a rear palm heel.

3. A quick eye rake immediately follows.

4. Next, a lead horizontal elbow.

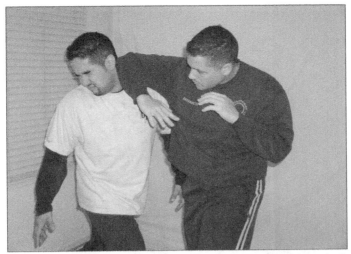

5. The compound attack is complete with a rear horizontal elbow.

COMPOUND ATTACK #12
(Finger Jab-Rear Cross-Head Butt-Vertical Knee)

1. Franco attempts to diffuse the situation.

105

2. He launches a finger jab to the opponent's eyes.

3. He follows up with a rear cross.

4. Franco engages the clinch with a head butt.

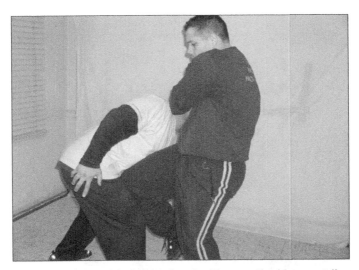

5. The adversary is neutralized with a vertical knee strike.

107

COMPOUND ATTACK #13
(Finger Jab-Web Hand Strike-Double Thumb Gouge-Rear Vertical Knee)

1. Franco assumes a de-escalation stance.

2. He launches a finger jab to the opponent's eyes.

3. Then follows up with a rear web hand strike to the throat.

4. Franco moves in with a double thumb gouge.

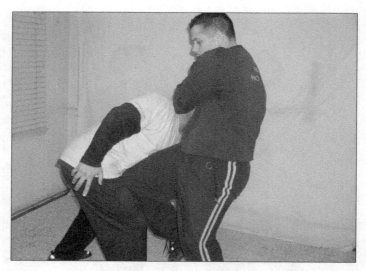

5. The adversary is neutralized with a vertical knee strike.

COMPOUND ATTACK #14
(Eye Rake-Rear Vertical Elbow-Head Butt)

1. Franco assumes a de-escalation stance.

2. Franco traps his opponent's hand and counters with an eye rake.

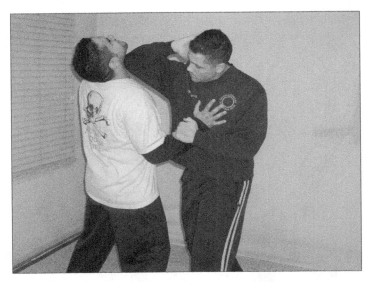

3. He follows with a rear vertical elbow strike.

111

4. Franco engages the clinch with a head butt.

COMPOUND ATTACK #15
(Rear Palm Heel-Double Thumb Gouge-Vertical Knee)

1. Franco (right) assumes a first strike stance.

2. He strikes first with a rear palm heel.

3. He follows up with a double thumb gouge.

113

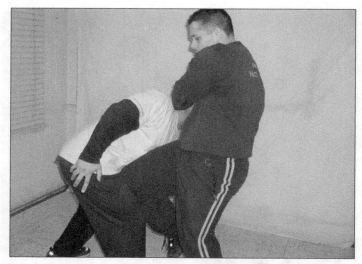

4. He completes his attack with a rear vertical knee strike.

COMPOUND ATTACK #16
(Finger Jab-Hook Punch-Lead Hook-Rear Uppercut)

1. Franco assumes a de-escalation stance.

2. He launches a finger jab to the opponent's eyes.

3. Followed by a rear hook punch.

4. The compound attack continues with a lead hook punch.

5. A rear uppercut to the chin ends the altercation.

COMPOUND ATTACK #17
(Push Kick-Hammer Fist-Rear Vertical Knee)

1. Franco de-escalates from the kicking range.

2. Franco launches a push kick to the opponent's thigh.

3. He follows up with a long arc hammer fist to the opponent's back.

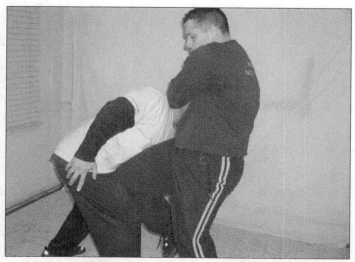

4. He completes his attack with a rear vertical knee strike.

COMPOUND ATTACK #18
(Web Hand Strike-Lead Hook-Rear Hook)

1. Franco (right) assumes a first strike stance.

2. Franco attacks with a rear web hand strike.

3. Next is a lead hook punch.

4. Followed by a rear hook punch.

COMPOUND ATTACK #19
(Web Hand-Horizontal Elbow-Uppercut-Head Butt)

1. Franco employs a de-escalation stance.

2. He strikes first with a rear web hand strike.

3. Then follows up with a lead horizontal elbow.

4. A rear uppercut is next.

5. Franco drops his opponent with a head butt.

COMPOUND ATTACK #20
(Push Kick-Uppercut-Vertical Knee)

1. Franco de-escalates from the kicking range.

2. Franco launches a push kick to the opponent's thigh.

3. Followed by a rear uppercut.

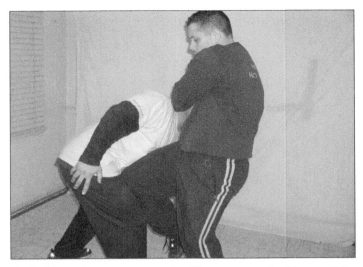

4. He finishes the adversary off with a rear vertical knee strike.

In many ways, your offensive skills must be comparable with a high-powered machine gun. During the course of your compound attack, it's imperative you overwhelm your adversary by showering him with a barrage of rapid, successive blows designed to both injure him and demolish his defenses. Do you have the necessary fire-power to neutralize your enemy?

125

CHAPTER FOUR
The Smell of the Grave

GROUND FIGHTING

Regardless of how skilled you may be with your striking arsenal, there's a very strong possibility that a combat situation will go to the ground. Actually, the majority of most fights usually end up on the ground. The bottom line is, if your adversary is truly determined to take you to the ground, he will most likely succeed. Therefore, it's critical that you have the knowledge, skills and attitude necessary to handle most ground fighting situations. You most possess a ground fighting arsenal which includes both submission techniques and natural body weapons.

Like all forms of combat, it's essential that you keep your head during the ground fight. Losing your temper or panicking when taken to the ground may cost you your life. However, "keeping your cool" will conserve energy and significantly reduce the possibility of tactical errors.

Lets first take a look at the five ground fighting positions. Once I introduce them to you, we can move forward with specific escape techniques and survival tactics. The basic ground fighting positions are as follows: the mounted position, perpendicular mount (head to head & chest to chest), the guard, opposite pole position and chest to back position.

If you're not prepared for a potential ground fight, you may be subjected to: (1) premature exhaustion (to the untrained, ground fighting is the most exhausting form of fighting), (2) panic, (3) injury or possible death, (4) humiliation, (5) defeat, and (6) suffocation.

129

Basic Ground Fighting Positions

Mounted Position - This is when you are sitting on top of the assailant's torso or chest. The fighter who establishes the top-mounted position has a tremendous advantage in the ground fight. From this position, you can deliver a variety of blows and yet be in a strategic position to avoid most counterstrikes. The mounted position also restricts your assailant's mobility and permits you to generate tremendous power.

When mounting your assailant, always try to sit above his hips and as close to his chest as possible. This is important for the following reasons: (1) it prevents the assailant from bumping you; (2) it places you closer to the assailant's facial targets so you can effectively strike them; (3) it brings you closer to the assailant's arms and throat for instantaneous submission holds and chokes; and (4) it helps marry his back to the floor.

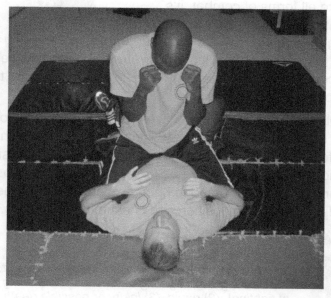

A student demonstrates the top mounted position.

Perpendicular Mount Position – This is when both of your legs are on one side of the opponent's body. Essentially, your body runs perpendicular to the adversary. There are two variations of the perpendicular mount: head to head and chest-to-chest.

Pictured here, the perpendicular mount position (head to head).

The perpendicular mount (chest to chest variation).

131

Guard Position - This is when you wrap both your legs around the assailant's waist. Although the guard is a defensive ground fighting position, you can perform a wide variety of chokes and holds. Brazilian Jujitsu systems are well known for their proficiency in this particular ground fighting position.

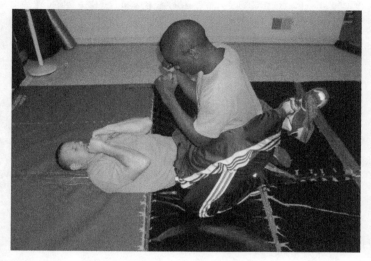

The fighter on the bottom demonstrates the "defensive" guard position. Notice how his hands are close to his face.

The only real way to learn ground fighting skills is to experience them. "Feeling" every movement is your first step to ground fighting mastery.

Opposite Pole Position - This is when both you and the grappler momentarily face opposite directions during the course of a ground fight. Believe it or not, this position occurs quite often in a ground struggle.

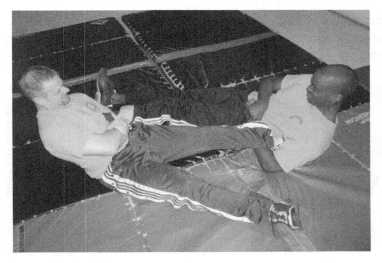

Both students demonstrate the opposite pole position.

One of the foundational elements of effective ground fighting is being able to move well on the floor. Ground fighting mobility is just as important as standing mobility.

Chest to Back Position – This is the *check mate* of all ground fighting positions. This is when your chest is against the opponent's back. One of the cardinal rules for ground fighting is, under no circumstances should you ever roll over onto your stomach and expose your back to your opponent!

The chest to back position is dangerous for your adversary because it's virtually impossible for him to defend himself. From this position, you could easily choke out your adversary or deliver a barrage of blows to his head, neck and back.

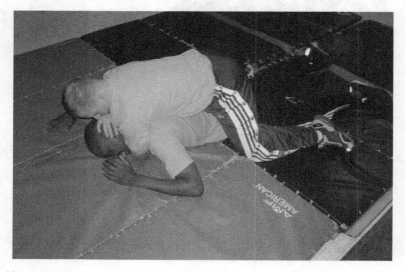

Here, the fighter on top demonstrates the chest to back position.

A good ground fighter can control and dominate his assailant by tactile feeling. "Tactile sight" is a critical attribute that will permit you to excel in the ground fight.

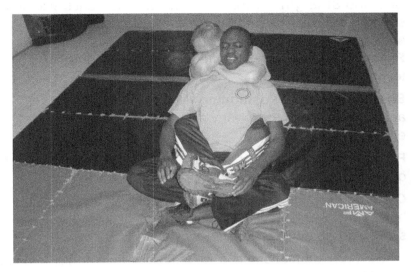

Pictured here, the chest to back position from a seated position.

Now that you have a fundamental understanding of the various ground fighting positions, it's time to learn a few basic submission holds. Submission techniques include a wide spectrum of holds and locks designed to make the opponent submit. Such techniques are to be used in fighting situations where lethal force is not warranted and justified (i.e. school yard fight, feuding relatives, drunk friend, bar fight, etc.) Such techniques are not designed to maim or terminate your assailant. However when properly applied, they will put him out of commission and allow you to safely escape.

However, before I begin, a few caveats must first be stated. First, while submission holds are a necessary component of your combative cache, never forget some of their inherent risks and limitations. Some include:

Somatotypes - many ground fighting maneuvers and techniques will not work effectively against large and anatomically flexible assailants.

135

Size and Strength - in some cases, your assailant's size and strength can often negate the effectiveness of certain submission holds.

Psychoactive drugs - will often nullify your submission techniques.

Exact Anatomical Positioning - you must have exact anatomical positioning for any submission technique to work effectively.

Frenetic Movements - your assailant's frenetic movements often makes it difficult to apply precise submission holds.

Clothing - you can't effectively employ certain submission holds when wearing thick or cumbersome clothing (i.e. rain slicker, goose down jackets, snow suit, etc.)

Second, when attempting a submission hold, never force it! If you have to "force" the technique, chances are it's tactically inappropriate for the situation. The correct application of a submission technique can only be found within a window of opportunity.

Generally, six elements must be present for a submission technique to be applied effectively: (1) The assailant's appendage is exposed and free from obstruction; (2) You are in the proper range to apply the technique; (3) You are in the correct position to apply the technique; (4) You have the most efficient angle of application; (5) Your submission technique does not place you in harm's way; (6) You must have the necessary leverage to effectively apply the technique.

Third, never forget the tactical limitations and disadvantages of ground fighting. They include but are not limited to the following:

Multiple Assailants - since ground fighting requires maximal body entanglement, it is virtually impossible to fight multiple attackers.

Edged Weapons - it is often difficult to defend against knives and other edged weapons when locked up with your assailant.

Spectator Intervention - spectator intervention can occur when you are locked up in a ground fight.

Positional Asphyxia - when ground fighting a heavier assailant, positional asphyxia can occur if you're not careful.

Terrain - the type of terrain you're ground fighting on can be dangerous - (i.e. broken glass, sharp metal, broken wood, etc.)

Environmental Dangers - your environment and immediate surrounding can harm you (i.e. heavy traffic, a cliff, the curb of the street, etc.)

Limited Vision - ground fighting can significantly inhibit your peripheral vision.

Limited Mobility - you cannot escape quickly when you are locked up in a ground fight.

Hand Grips for Ground Combat

The foundation of most submission holds are predicated on your hand grip. There are many different types of hand grips. Here are four that you should know:

Three-finger grip - join your hands together and place your thumb between the index and middle finger of your other hand, then clasp your hands together.

Knife-hand grip - join your hands together by grasping the knife edge of your other hand.

Wrist grip - join your hands together by grasping the wrist of your other hand.

Indian grip - join your hands together, locking and curling your fingers into both palms.

4 Hand Grips for Ground Combat

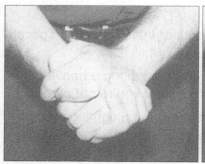

Three Finger Grip

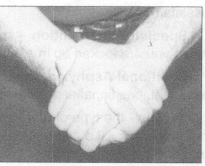

Knife-Hand Grip

Wrist Grip

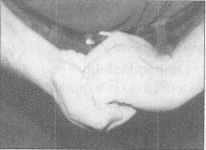

Indian Grip

Now that you have an understanding of the basics, let's take a look at a few submission holds that should be added to your ground fighting arsenal. We will start with the box technique.

Never use a full-hand grip. This grip is inadequate because it separates your thumb too much from your other four fingers. This weakens the structural integrity of your grip, thus allowing your assailant to escape your hold. Use the Indian grip instead.

THE BOX

This is a painful submission hold that can be applied when you have perpendicularly or vertically mounted the assailant. Injury and damage is applied to the assailant's shoulder.

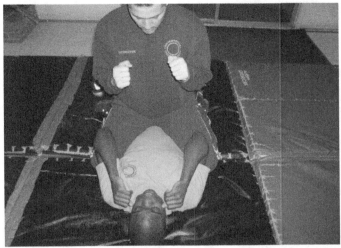

1. Sammy Franco (top) starts from the top mounted position.

2. Before applying the submission hold, Franco first weakens his adversary with an elbow strike.

3. Once the adversary is stunned, Franco quickly grabs the assailant's right wrist with his right hand (making certain his right hand is held in the thumb over position).

4. Next, Franco inserts his left hand underneath the assailant's right arm and on top of his right wrist. Once the hold is positioned, Franco raises the assailant's right elbow and drags his hand down toward his legs. Be certain to keep the assailant's wrist on the floor as you drag his arm downwards. Notice how Sammy keeps his face and head tucked away.

PARTY FLEX

This is another painful submission hold that can be applied when you have perpendicularly or vertically mounted the assailant. Damage and injury is applied to the assailant's wrist.

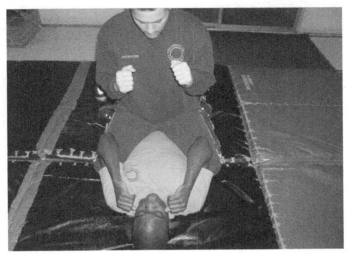

1. Franco (top) starts from the top mounted position.

2. Before applying the submission hold, Franco first weakens his adversary with an elbow strike.

141

3. After striking, Franco stabilizes the assailant's elbow with his right hand. Also note how Franco keeps his head safely tucked away.

4. Once the elbow is stable, Franco grabs the assailant's right hand and flexes it downward to the ground.

MODIFIED JAPANESE ARM BAR

This is a versatile submission hold applied when your assailant unknowingly offers you an outstretched arm. Damage and injury is applied to the assailant's elbow.

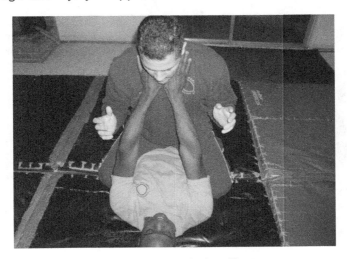

1. The adversary chokes Franco.

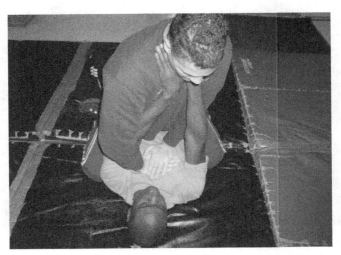

2. Franco places both of his palms on the assailant's chest (making certain the assailant's left arm is between both of his arms).

143

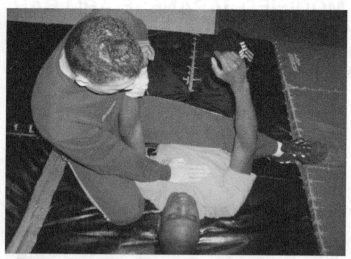

3. Without telegraphing his movements, he pushes off the assailant's chest and lifts his entire body up and around the assailant's torso. He simultaneously grabs hold of the assailant's left wrist with his hand, stretching it out as he falls back.

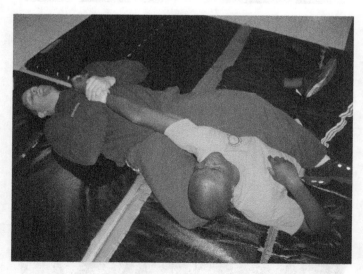

4. Once Franco lands on the ground, he marries the opponent's left wrist to his chest. Notice how Franco's body runs perpendicular to the assailant's torso. To inflict pain on the assailant's elbow, simultaneously arch your back.

5. In this photograph, Franco demonstrates a wicked variation of the Modified Japanese Arm Bar, called the CRUCIFIX.

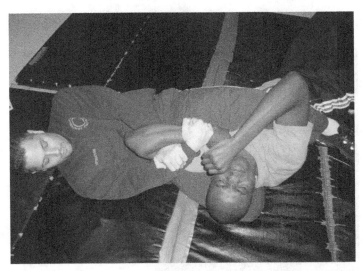

6. Here, Franco demonstrates the "figure four modification." This technique is often used when the adversary curls his arm inward to counter your modified Japanese arm bar.

FOREARM CHOKE

This is a very effective choking technique applied from the top mounted position. Damage and injury is applied to the assailant's throat.

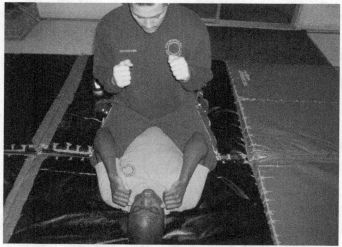

1. Franco (top) starts from the top mounted position.

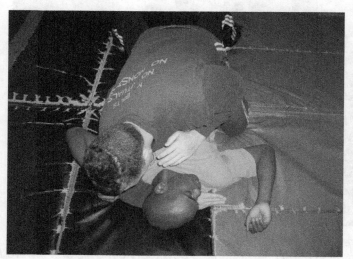

2. From the mounted position, Franco places his right forearm behind the assailant's neck (blade side facing his neck).

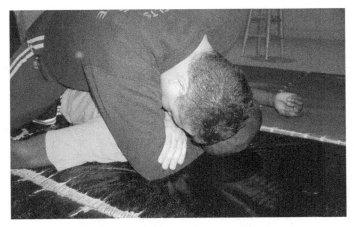

3. Next, he inserts the web of his left hand into the crook of his right forearm. Then places the blade side of his left firearm into the assailant's windpipe.

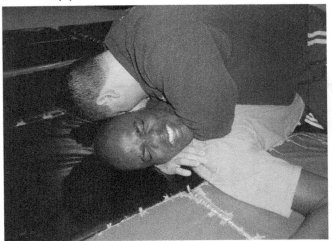

4. Franco drops his weight on his adversary and compresses and scissors both of his forearms into one another

WARNING: The forearm choke can easily crush the assailant's windpipe, causing death. This ground fighting technique should only be used in life and death situations when lethal force is warranted and justified.

Important Reminder: Make certain to employ the double leg grapevine when applying the forearm choke. This will prevent your adversary from bumping you out of the mounted position.

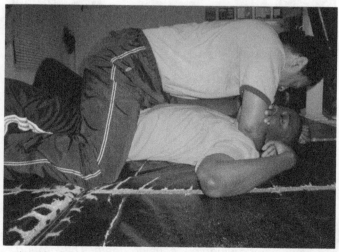

Here, the student on top demonstrates a poor base. Notice how there's too much room between him and his opponent. He could easily be knocked off from the top mounted position.

NAKED CHOKE

This is a very effective choking technique applied from the chest to back position. Damage and injury is applied to the assailant's throat. WARNING: The naked choke can crush the assailant's windpipe, causing death. This ground fighting technique should only be used in life and death situations when lethal force is warranted and justified.

1. Franco begins from the chest to back position.

2. Next, he stretches his arm in front of the assailant with his palm facing down.

3. Franco places the assailant's windpipe in the crook of his right elbow and simultaneously grabs his shirt with his right hand.

4. Place the blade side of your left forearm into the assailant's neck, with your hand behind his head. With both arms, slowly squeeze the lateral sides of the assailant's neck, scissoring your elbows together.

5. Common mistakes to avoid with the Naked Choke are inserting the hand into the crook of the bicep, and placing you hand on top of the opponent's head.

GUILLOTINE

This is a very effective choking technique applied from the guard position. Damage and injury is applied to the assailant's throat. WARNING: The guillotine choke can crush the assailant's windpipe, causing death.

1. The student begins on his back in the guard position.

151

2. Next, he uses his legs to pull his adversary towards him and simultaneously reaches around his neck with his right arm.

3. The practitioner solidifies his hold with an Indian grip and simultaneously pulls the opponent's head from his shoulders. NOTE: Be certain to use your legs to help pull your adversary away from you.

BODY WEAPON TOOLS

Natural body weapons are another essential component of your ground fighting arsenal. You body weapon arsenal includes the following tools and techniques: tight linear punches, hammer fist strikes, biting, eye gouging and raking, fingers breaks, and throat crushing. Let take a look at some of them.

Tight Linear Punches

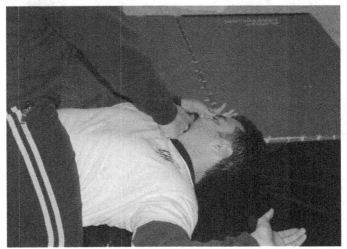

Once your balance is established in the mounted position, you can proceed with a vicious flurry of strikes delivered to the opponent's face – this is known as pummeling. Punching from this position is extremely effective because you have the gravitational advantage and the grappler's head is flush against the floor (the floor functions as a stabilizer that concentrates your impact). The best blows for the pummel assault are tight linear punches, hammer fists, and in some cases elbow strikes.

WARNING! Be careful, pummeling from the top mounted position can be deadly. Always be certain that your actions are legally warranted and justified.

Finger Breaking

Another effective ground fighting tactic is breaking the grappler's fingers. It's quick, efficient and can be employed while you are standing, kneeling and lying in various ground fighting positions.

The grappler's fingers are ideal targets - if you break his fingers or injure his hands he will have a very difficult time grappling with you. In this photograph, Franco (bottom) rips his opponent's finger backwards.

Broken fingers also makes it very difficult for your adversary to deliver punching blows during a ground fight. Consider adding it to your ground fighting arsenal.

154

Crushing Tactics

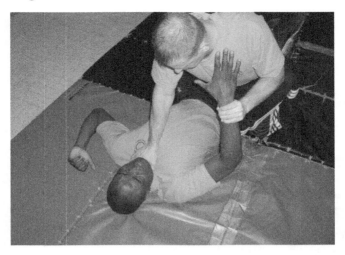

When faced with deadly force situations, you want the quickest and most efficient method of terminating the grappler. One brutal "nuclear technique" is crushing.

Crushing techniques work especially well when the grappler's body is anchored against the floor. Crushing the assailant's throat is not an easy task. It requires quick and exact digit placement, sufficient leverage accompanied with the vicious determination to destroy your assailant.

 *Nuclear ground fighting techniques are designed to inflict immediate and irreversible damage, rendering the criminal assailant helpless. Some nuclear tools and tactics include: (1) biting, (2) tearing, (3) crushing, (4) long-term choking, (5) gouging, (6) raking, and (7) all striking techniques.*

155

Biting Tactics

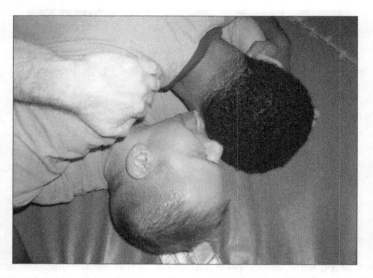

Biting can be very effective when fighting a grappler on the floor. When biting your adversary, it's important to penetrate deep and hard with your molars and shake your head vigorously back and forth. Not only is biting effective on a physical level, it also transmits a strong psychological message to the assailant.

BEWARE! Biting should only be used as a last resort; you run the risk of contracting AIDS if your attacker is infected and you draw blood while biting him.

Tactical biting is a game changer during a ground fight. That's why I've created an entire fighting methodology called "Savage Street Fighting", available in both book and video format.

Gouging Tactics

Driving your fingers into the grappler's eyes is another effective method of controlling a ground fight. However, be forewarned, some grapplers are very capable of ground fighting without the use of vision (assuming they're not in excruciating pain).

The ability to ground fight with the adversary while blinded cannot be overstated. That's why I encourage all my students to ground fight while blindfolded.

157

ESCAPE TECHNIQUES

Submission holds and striking tactics alone won't prepare you for the uncertain conditions of a ground fight. You must also possess the skill and ability to escape from a variety of positions. What follows are just a few examples.

ESCAPING FROM THE MOUNT

1. The adversary mounts the practitioner.

2. The practitioner traps the opponent's right arm and leg.

3. Once the opponent's arms and legs are trapped, the practitioner thrusts his hips upwards and rolls to his left.

4. Once the practitioner successfully escapes the mounted position, he ends up in his opponent's leg guard. Keep in mind that your average street thug will NOT place you in a guard position after you bump them from the top mounted position. However, an adversary who is well versed in ground fighting tactics will most likely employ the guard position.

5. Notice how the practitioner (top) leans back when placed in his opponent's guard. Leaning back is important for several reasons. First, it prevents your assailant from pulling you down and embracing you. Second, it offers you the range and angle to repeatedly strike the grappler's groin or strike the grappler's face if he decides to reach and grab you. Finally, it puts you into a position to escape from grappler's leg guard.

While most MMA fighters prefer to fight from the guard position, it's not ideal for street combat where conditions are often unfair and unpredictable.

ESCAPING FROM THE GUARD

In order to safely escape the grappler's leg guard, you must first weaken him with various striking and biting techniques. The next series of photographs will illustrate this point.

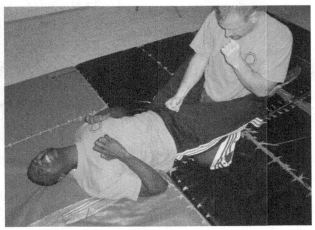

1. Hammering the opponent's groin with your fists is another effective way of getting him to release his guard. Notice how the striker (top) leans back for both range and leverage.

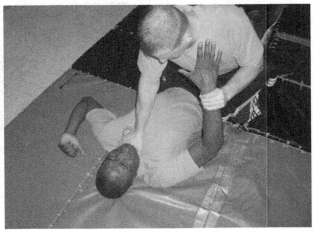

2. If the situation warrants, you can counter the grappler's guard with a throat crush. Be certain that your actions and justified in the eyes of the law!

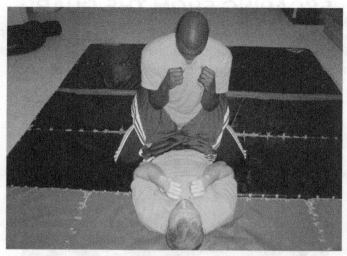

3. Once you have weakened the adversary with strikes, you will need a few seconds to escape from his guard. Begin, by leaning back and positioning both of your elbow points on the lower inside area of his thighs (by his knees).

4. Here, the practitioner (top) climbs out of the opponent's guard and begins to mount him. Notice that he keeps his hands up to defend against a possible strike.

PERPENDICULAR MOUNT ESCAPE

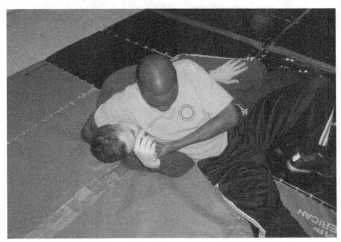

1. If you find yourself placed in a side headlock from a perpendicular mount position, it's critical that your arms are not trapped behind the opponent's back. In this photo, the author (bottom) demonstrates that his right arm is free to apply the counter.

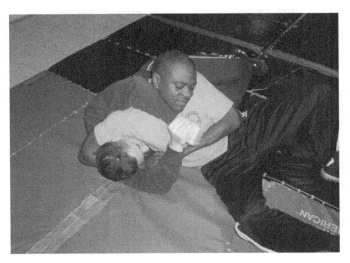

2. This is the correct hand placement when defending against a side headlock from a perpendicular mount position. Notice how Franco's hands are in front of the grappler's chest. This allows him to secure the "box frame" position against the grappler's throat.

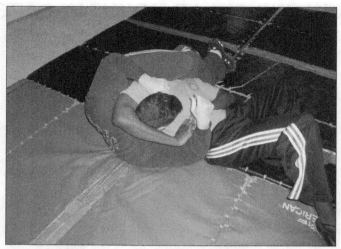

3. Once the box frame is secured, Franco walks backwards and rocks the grappler backward into his legs where a leg choke counter awaits the adversary.

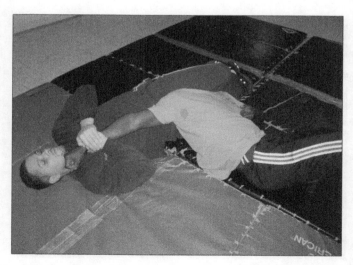

4. After the leg choke is secure, Franco straightens his body out and finishes the grappler off with a straight-arm bar.

ANATOMICAL HANDLES

Effective ground fighting skills require an understanding of the assailant's anatomical handles. Anatomical handles are various body parts (i.e., appendages, joints, and in some cases, organs) that can be grabbed, held, pulled or otherwise manipulated during the course of a ground fight.

There are numerous anatomical handles, and they include the following: hair, eye sockets, nose, chin, jaw, ears, throat, neck, elbows, wrists, arms, back of knees, ankles, and hip region.

The most common anatomical handle is the opponent's wrist.

Keep your hair short, especially at the back of your head. Long hair or trendy ponytails can be dangerous and risky because your assailant can easily pull and control you during the ground fight.

165

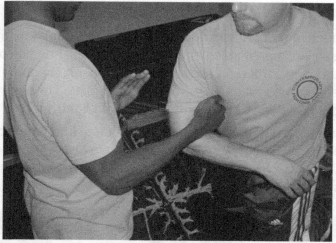

The opponent's arms are also excellent anatomical handles.

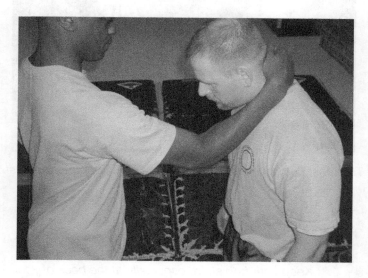

Another very effective anatomical handle for ground fighting is the opponent's neck.

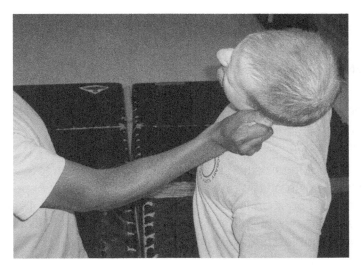

You'd be amazed how much control you have over your adversary by grabbing his ear.

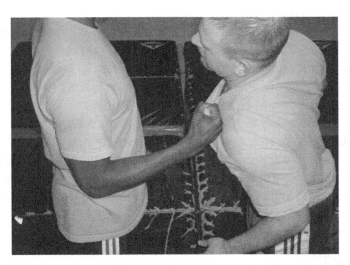

Your opponent doesn't have to be wearing a Ju-jitsu gi for you to grab hold of him. In some circumstances, your typical t-shirt will do just fine.

MORE GROUND FIGHTING TIPS

MOUNT THE ADVERSARY IMMEDIATELY

If and when the street fight does go down to the ground, immediately try to mount your adversary. Remember that the fighter who establishes the mounted position has a tremendous tactical advantage in the ground fight.

The mounted position is the "cockpit" from which to effectively finish off the grappler. The most important aspect of the mounted position is that it puts you in position to deliver a variety of blows and submission holds, yet it is very difficult for your assailant to effectively counter or escape.

USE YOUR ENVIRONMENT

Once you've established the mounted position, you can also take advantage of your environment and use it to your advantage. Here are just a few good examples. Drive or smash the assailant's head or face into the pavement or curb of the street. This is often referred to as a "curbie." If the situation presents itself, force your assailant's head under water, sand, snow, thick mud, a pile of wet leaves for a prolonged period of time. Or shove your adversary's head or eyes into broken glass, thrust your assailant's eyes, or head into barb wire or razor wire, or maneuver your assailant's entire head into the pathway of moving machinery. WARNING: This type of environmental exploitation should only be used in life and death encounters where lethal force is warranted and justified in the eyes of the law.

TAIL SPIN

There might be a time when you are thrown to the ground and the opponent is standing above you. While he does have the tactical advantage, you can use the tail spin technique to get yourself out of trouble. The tail spin is executed by first chambering one of your legs back (to launch a kick) then pivoting and rotating your body in the direction of the adversary. Quick pivoting can be accomplished by spinning on your butt while your elbows maintain your balance.

The tailspin, accompanied with a kick, will keep the grappler back and temporarily prevent him from either mounting, rushing, jumping, or kicking you. The objective of the kick is to get him back so that you can quickly get back on your feet. You can launch your kick while lying on your side or your back.

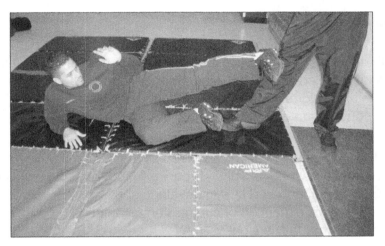

In this photo, the author uses the tail spin technique to launch his kick. Notice that he keeps his left arm up.

PRACTICE REGULARLY

To be truly prepared for the grappler, you must engage in rigorous and frequent ground fighting with a trustworthy training partner. Some important skills to focus on are: chokes, finger breaks, throat crushing, biting, pummeling, various submission holds, maintaining the mounted position, escaping the assailant's guard, escaping the mounted position, defending against the pummel, escaping from the side head lock, escape from various submission holds and chokes, establishing the mounted position, establishing the perpendicular mount, and maintaining the perpendicular mount.

Due to the very nature of ground fighting training, there is always the possibility of injuries. Therefore, considerable attention must be given to safety. Here are a few tips and suggestions to keep injuries at a minimum. Warm up prior to ground fighting sessions; keep your fingernails well trimmed; don't wear jewelry during training sessions, practice with a training partner whom you can trust and who can control his techniques.

You should also experience what it is like to ground fight with different types of weapons. Experiment and see what it's like to grapple with edged weapons (use training knives only), sticks and bludgeons, and various types of makeshift weapons. Try to ground fight while blind folded. This is important for the several reasons.

First, it helps you develop a keen sense of kinesthetic awareness. Second, it helps prepare you to ground fight while visually handicapped. Third, it develops anatomical orientation allowing quick execution of submission techniques. Fourth, it cultivates your tactile sight.

Moreover, if you want to be exceptionally prepared for the possible ground fight, you'll need to also experience what it's like to fight with only one arm. Find a trustworthy partner with whom you can work with (he can use both arms but you can only use one). This type of training is important for several reasons.

First, it physically and psychologically prepares you to fight while handicapped. Second, it enhances your appendage awareness when ground fighting. Third, it reinforces efficient and economical tactics and techniques. Finally, it builds ground fighting confidence.

170

The unfortunate fact about grappling combat is that you may be faced with more than one adversary. Therefore it's imperative that you experience what it's like to ground fight two assailants at the same time. This type of training can be conducted while you and your training partners are standing, kneeling or lying in the prone position. Remember: It's important that your training partners know how to work with you through the training session.

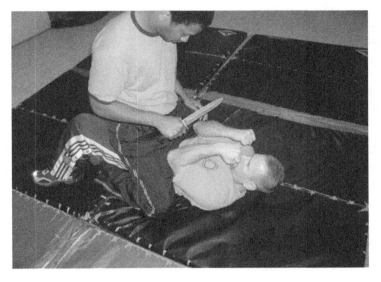

Ground fighting against a knife-wielding attacker is critical for anyone interested in reality based self-defense training.

Very few grappling and ground fighting practitioners are prepared to ground fight against an edged weapon, make it a priority in your self-defense training.

171

CHAPTER FIVE
Uncontrollable

ESCAPING CHOKES, LOCK & HOLDS

Being placed in a throat choke, bear hug or any restraint for that matter can startle someone with little or no training. In most cases, it's not the choke, lock or hold that defeats the victim, it's the panic. For this reason alone, you should always remain calm and relaxed so you can accurately assess the danger and respond accordingly to the situation.

Whenever you are placed in a choke, you must react immediately before the criminal attacker can apply any significant amount of pressure. A good rule of thumb is to never match muscle against muscle by forcefully wrestling your way out of the restraint. This will only waste valuable time and energy and may even enhance the effectiveness of the opponent's attack.

Keep in mind that if your assailant has you in a hold or choke, then his hands and arms will most likely be occupied and he will be unable to defend against your counterattack.

Escaping from various chokes and holds requires quick, intuitive reaction. It must be second nature the instant you feel contact with the adversary.

175

TWO-HAND WRIST GRAB ESCAPE
(high grab)

1. Franco assumes a de-escalation stance.

2. The adversary grabs both of Franco's wrists.

3. To escape from the grab, Franco raises his right hand up and over his left and quickly retracts his arm.

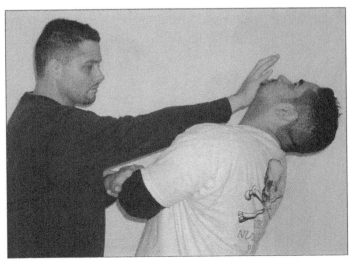

4. Once his right hand is free, he counters with a rear palm heel strike to the chin.

177

TWO-HAND WRIST GRAB ESCAPE
(low grab)

1. The adversary grabs both of Franco's wrists.

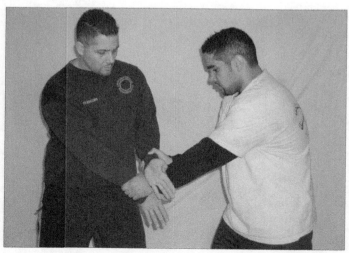

2. To escape from the grab, Franco (left) places his left hand over his opponent's wrists.

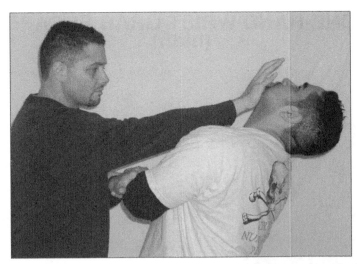

3. Franco pulls his right hand out and counters with a rear palm heel strike to the chin.

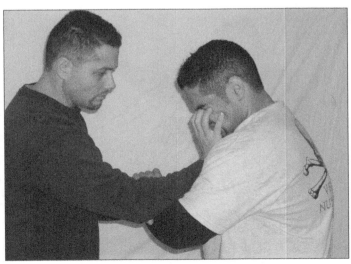

4. He follows up with an eye rake.

ONE-HAND WRIST GRAB ESCAPE
(high)

1. The adversary grabs Franco's wrist.

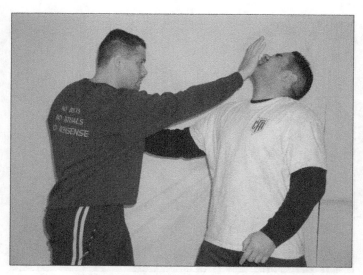

2. Franco immediately counters with a palm heel strike.

FRONT SHIRT GRAB COUNTER

1. In this photo, the opponent grabs Franco's shirt. Franco slowly raises his hands and attempts to de-escalate the situation.

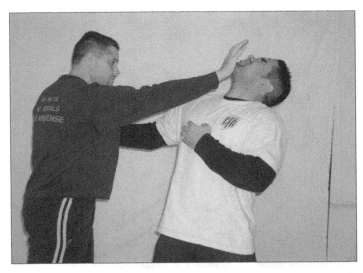

2. Without telegraphing his intention, Franco slams a rear palm heel into his opponent's chin.

SHOULDER GRAB COUNTER

1. *The assailant grabs Franco's left shoulder and prepares to launch an attack.*

2. *Franco swings his left arm around his opponent's arm and traps it.*

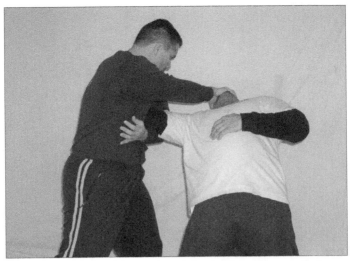

3. He counters with a palm strike to the opponent's face.

CHEST POKE COUNTER

1. The assailant threatens and pokes Franco in the chest. Franco sets up the counter by slowly raising both his arms.

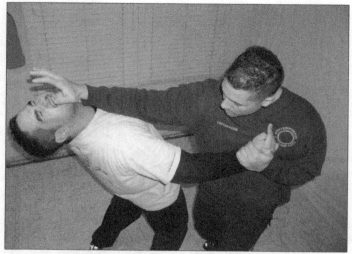

2. Franco simultaneously traps the opponent's wrist and counters with a palm heel strike.

FINGER IN FACE COUNTER

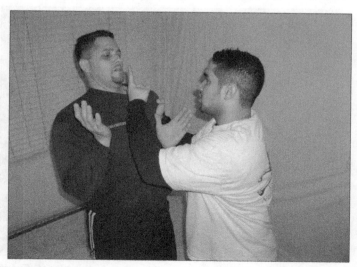

1. The assailant grabs Franco's shirt and sticks his finger in is face. Franco assumes the de-escalation stance.

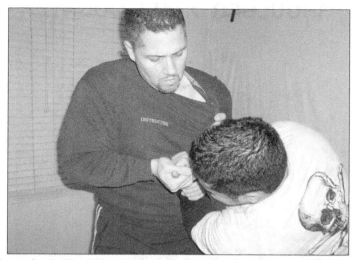

2. He grabs hold of his opponent's wrist and simultaneously breaks his index finger.

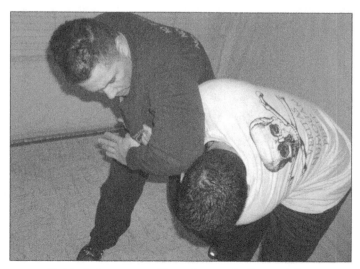

3. He follows up with a diagonal elbow strike.

185

SHOULDER DRAPE COUNTER

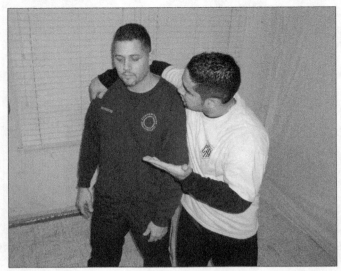

1. The adversary places his arm over Franco's shoulder and threatens him.

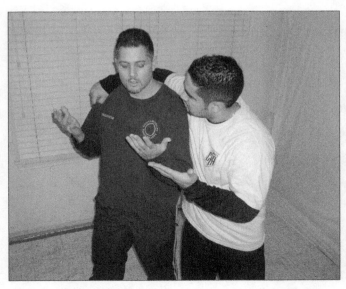

2. Franco sets up his counter by slowly raising both his arms.

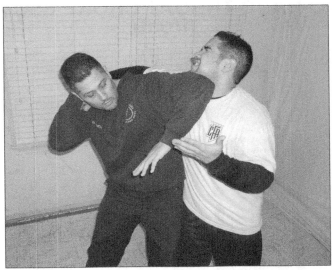

3. At the ideal moment, he traps his opponent's hand and drives a vertical elbow to the opponent's chin.

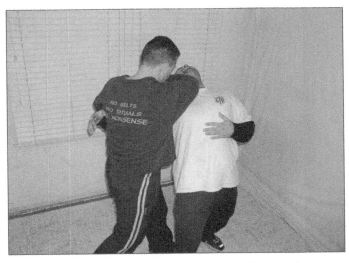

4. Franco follows up with another elbow strike.

TWO-HAND THROAT CHOKE ESCAPE
(front)

1. *The adversary chokes Franco with both hands.*

2. *Franco steps back with his right leg and simultaneously swings his left arm over the opponent's arms.*

3. *He whips his hips and counters with a tight elbow strike.*

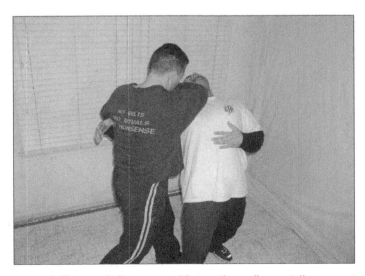

4. *Franco follows up with another elbow strike.*

REAR BEAR HUG ESCAPE

1. Franco is grabbed from behind.

2. To prevent himself from being lifted in the air, Franco bumps his hips backward and repeatedly smashes his opponent's hands with his knuckles.

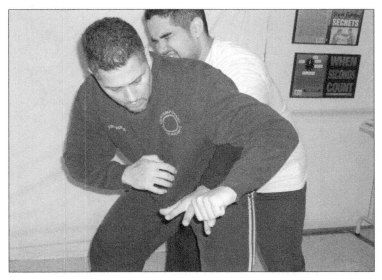

3. Once his adversary loosens his grip, he snatches his finger and breaks it.

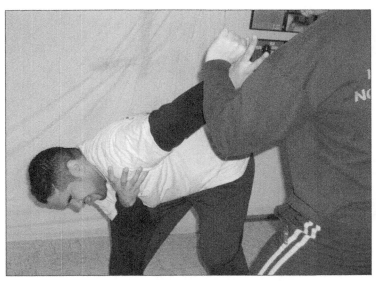

4. Franco spins his body out of the hold.

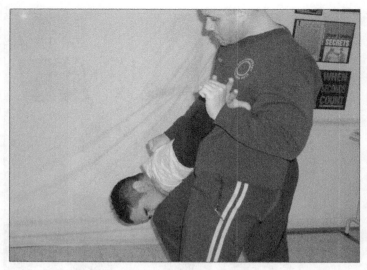

5. He finishes his adversary off with a knee strike to the face.

REAR BEAR HUG ESCAPE
(Arms pinned)

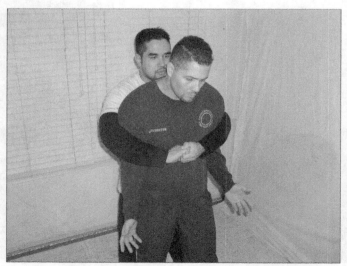

1. Franco is grabbed from behind, except this time his arms are pinned to his sides.

2. He grabs hold of his opponent's hands and bumps his hips back to stabilize his balance.

3. Franco steps to his side and strikes the assailant's groin.

4. He follows up with a vertical elbow strike to the solar plexus.

FRONT BEAR HUG ESCAPE

1. Franco is placed in a front bear hug.

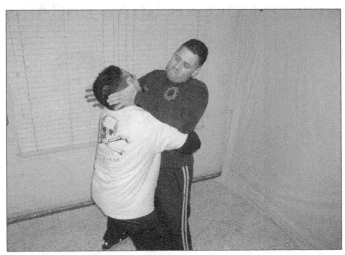

2. He counters by slamming both palms into his opponent's ears.

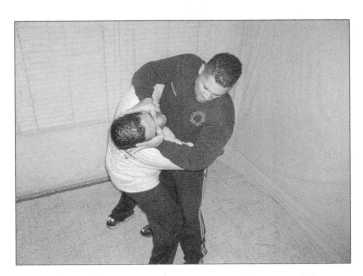

3. Then follows up with a double thumb gouge to the eyes.

REAR COLLAR GRAB ESCAPE

1. Franco is grabbed from behind.

2. He breaks the opponent's grab by stepping forward and circling his left arm around both his opponent's arms.

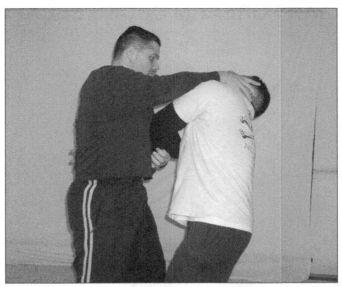

3. *Once Franco controls his opponent's arms, he counterattacks with an eye rake.*

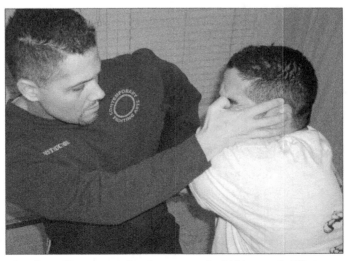

4. *Notice how Franco maintains control of his assailant's arms while executing the eye rake.*

REAR FOREARM CHOKE ESCAPE

1. Franco is choked from behind.

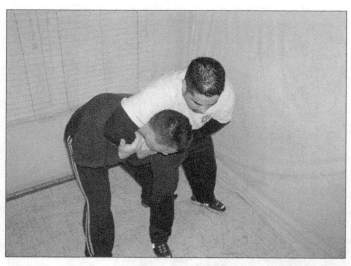

2. He grabs hold of his opponent's arm and stabilizes his balance. Next, he steps behind his adversary and turn his head inward.

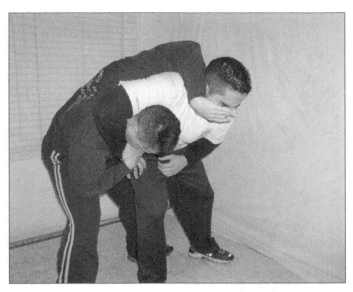

3. Franco reaches from behind and places his middle finger under his opponent's septum.

4. He pulls his adversary backwards.

5. Franco counters with extreme prejudice. Remember, attacking the assailant's throat must only be used when lethal force is warranted and justified in the eyes of the law.

SIDE HEAD LOCK ESCAPE

1. Franco is placed in a side headlock. He widens his leg base and simultaneously turns his head inward to keep his air passage open.

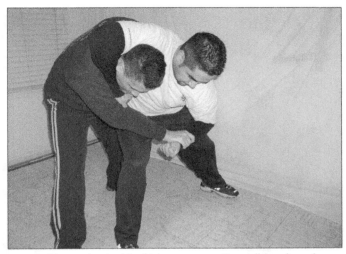

2. He grabs hold of his opponent's striking hand.

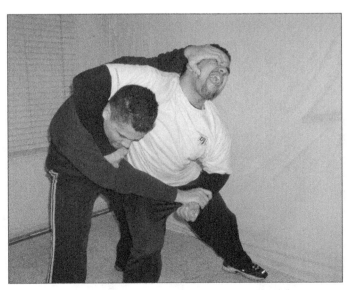

3. While maintaining control of his opponent's arm, Franco reaches from behind and attacks the eyes.

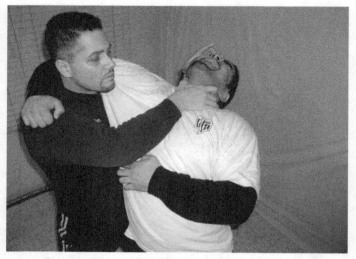

4. *While pulling the adversary backwards, he attacks attacks with a throat crush.*

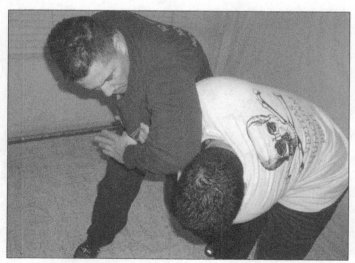

5. *Franco follows up with a diagonal elbow strike.*

CHAPTER SIX
Disobedient Defense

SEVEN COMPONENTS OF DEFENSE

In street combat, there's always the possibility that your adversary will launch a surprise attack and you'll have no choice but to *temporarily* resort to defensive tactics.

In the War Machine program, there are seven components of defense that must be mastered. They include the following:

1. Stances - the strategic posture you assume prior to or during combat.

2. Distance - the spatial relationship between you and your adversary.

3. Mobility - the ability to move your body quickly and freely while balanced.

4. Blocking - your various defensive tools designed to intercept your assailant's oncoming blow.

5. Parrying - your various defensive tools that redirect your assailant's blows.

6. Evading - defensive maneuvers designed to strategically move you away from your assailant's blow.

7. Attacking - offensive action designed to physically control, injure, cripple, or kill your assailant(s).

STANCES

As I mentioned in my first WAR MACHINE book, a skilled self-defense technician will never stand squarely in front of his adversary. If the opportunity presents itself, he will always try to assume a strategic stance or posture. A stance defines your ability to defend or attack you adversary and it can play a material role in the outcome of any self-defense altercation.

Stances are crucial in combat because it minimizes target exposure, enhances balance, promotes mobility, and significantly increases striking power. It's worth mentioning that while a stance is an essential component of combat, there might be some situations that will not afford you the luxury of assuming a stance. So always be prepared to deploy your offensive and defensive techniques without any foundational structure. Having said that, lets begin with the natural stance.

NATURAL STANCE

The natural stance is used when approached by an individual (i.e., drunken bum, street vagrant, typical stranger, etc.) who appears non-threatening, yet suspicious.

To assume this stance, angle your body 45-degrees from the suspicious individual and keep both of your feet approximately shoulder-width apart. Your knees should be slightly bent with your weight evenly distributed. Keep both of your hands in front of your body with some type of natural movement (e.g., rub your hands together, scratch your wrist, or scratch your temple), which will help protect your upper targets from a possible attack. Do remember to stay relaxed but alert, avoiding any muscular tension in your shoulders, neck, or arms.

When assuming a natural stance, never drop your hands to your sides; put your hands in your pockets or cross your arms. Keeping your hands down at your sides won't provide you with the necessary reaction time to defend against your assailant's attack effectively.

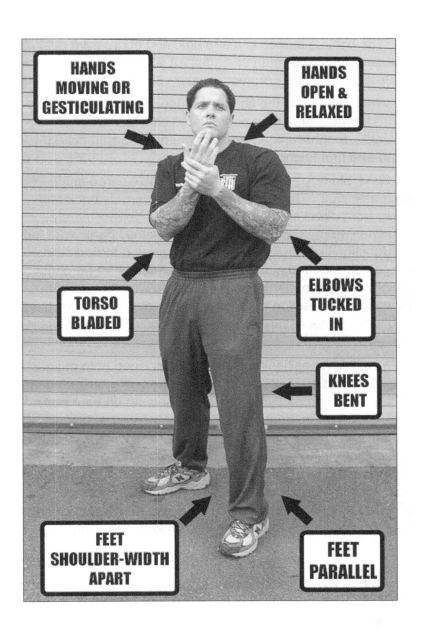

HANDS MOVING OR GESTICULATING

HANDS OPEN & RELAXED

TORSO BLADED

ELBOWS TUCKED IN

KNEES BENT

FEET SHOULDER-WIDTH APART

FEET PARALLEL

FIGHTING STANCE

The fighting stance is a strategic and aggressive posture that facilitates maximum execution of your compound attack while simultaneously protecting your vital anatomical targets.

When assuming the fighting stance, be certain to place your strongest and most coordinated side forward. For example, a right-handed person would stand with his right hand and foot facing his adversary.

Next, blade your feet and body at a 45-degree angle from your assailant. This will keep your body targets back and away from direct strikes. Place your feet approximately shoulder-width apart, with both knees slightly bent. Your legs will function like power springs to launch you through the ranges of unarmed combat. Try to maintain a 50-percent weight distribution. This will provide you with the ability to move in any direction quickly and efficiently, while providing you with the necessary stability to defend against various strikes.

Your hand positioning is also critical. Keep both of your hands up and align your lead hand in front of your rear hand. This will help protect your centerline and set up your body weapons. Your hands should be loosely fisted with your fingers curled and your wrists straight. This will prevent muscular tension and help increase the speed of your offensive and defensive movements. When holding your hand guard, make certain not to tighten your neck, shoulders or arms. Also, keep your chin angled down. This reduces the likelihood of a blow to the chin or a strike to the windpipe.

When assuming a fighting stance, try to align both your rear and lead hands. This will protect your centerline, temporarily negate the assailant's linear assault, and set up your body weapons.

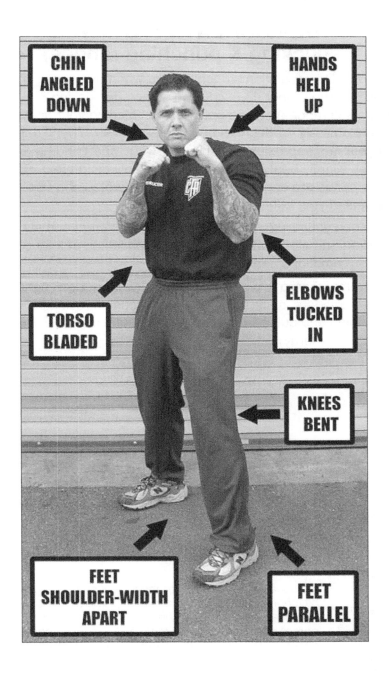

DE-ESCALATION STANCE
(kicking & punching ranges)

The De-escalation stance is used when diffusing a hostile person. The proper de-escalation stance (for kicking & punching ranges) can be acquired first blading your body at approximately 45-degrees from the adversary. Then keep both of your feet approximately shoulder-width apart and have your knees slightly bent with your weight evenly distributed. Both of your hands are open, relaxed, and up to protect the upper targets of your centerline.

Keep your torso, pelvis, head, and back erect and stay relaxed and alert—while remaining at ease and in total control of your emotions and body.

Remember to avoid any muscular tension—don't tighten up your shoulders, neck, arms, or thighs (tension restricts breathing and quick evasive movement, and it will quickly sap your vital energy).

De-escalation is a delicate mixture of science and art, psychology and warfare. It requires you to use both verbal and nonverbal techniques to calm the hostile person, while employ ing tactically deceptive physical safeguards to create the appearance that you are totally non aggressive.

DE-ESCALATION STANCE
(grappling range)

The De-escalation stance for grappling range is accomplished by first blading your body at approximately 45-degrees from the adversary. Then keep both of your feet approximately shoulder-width apart, knees slightly bent, and your weight evenly distributed. Place both of your hands side-by-side with your hands open, relaxed, and up to protect the upper gates of your centerline.

Keep your torso, pelvis, head, and back erect and stay relaxed and alert—while remaining at ease and in total control of your emotions and body. Remember to avoid any muscular tension—don't tighten up your shoulders, neck, arms, or thighs (tension restricts breathing and quick evasive movement, and it will quickly sap your vital energy).

One of the elements that separate reality based self-defense from every other martial arts style or system is the application of a de-escalation principles.

212

FIRST STRIKE STANCE
(kicking & punching ranges)

The first strike stance (kicking & punching range) is used prior to initiating a first strike in a fight. It facilitates "invisible deployment" of a preemptive strike while simultaneously protecting your vital targets against various possible counter attacks.

When assuming the first strike stance, have both of your feet approximately shoulder-width apart, knees slightly bent with your body weight evenly distributed over each leg. Blade your body at a 45-degree angle from your adversary. This position will help situate your centerline at a protective angle from your opponent, enhance your balance, promote mobility and set up your first strike weapons. Next, make certain to keep your torso, pelvis, head and back straight. And always stay relaxed and ready. Don't make the mistake of tensing your neck, shoulders, arms or thighs. This muscular tension will most certainly throw off your timing, retard the speed of your movements, and telegraph your intentions.

Your hand positioning is another critical component of the first strike stance. When confronted with an opponent in the kicking and punching ranges of unarmed combat, keep both of your hands open, relaxed and up to protect the upper gates of your centerline. Both of your palms should be facing the opponent with your lead arm bent between 90 and 120 degrees while your rear arm should be approximately 8 inches from your chin. When faced with an opponent in grappling range, keep both of your hands side by side of one another.

Your eyes are not deceiving you; the first strike stance is identical to the de-escalation stance. The only difference is your intent.

Here, the author (right) assumes a first strike stance in the punching range of unarmed combat.

Without telegraphing his intentions, Franco delivers a preemptive strike to his opponent's chin.

KNIFE DEFENSE STANCE

Defending against an edged-weapon attack requires mastery of the knife-defense stance. This protective stance will ensure maximal mobility and minimal target exposure, while simultaneously facilitating immediate counterstrike ability.

To assume the knife defense stance, first angle your body (internal organs) approximately 45-degrees from your enemy. Second, slightly hunch your shoulders forward and let your stomach sink in while keeping your head and face back and away from random slashes or stabs. Third, keep your hands, forearms, and elbows close to your body to diminish target opportunities for your assailant.

Remember to cup your hands with your palms facing you, which will turn soft tissue, veins, and arteries in the arms away from the blade. Also keep your knees slightly bent and flexible with your feet shoulder-width apart, and your weight equally distributed on each leg.

When assuming the knife defense stance, be certain to keep your internal organs away from the blade. Also remember to cup your hands with your palms facing you, which will turn soft tissue, veins, and arteries in the arms away from the edged weapon.

SHOULDERS SLIGHTLY HUNCHED

HANDS CUPPED & PALMS FACING YOU

STOMACH SUNK IN

ELBOWS TUCKED IN

KNEES BENT

FEET SHOULDER-WIDTH APART

FEET PARALLEL

KNIFE FIGHTING STANCE

The knife fighting stance is used when both you and your adversary are armed with a knife or similar edged weapon, such as a shard of glass, broken bottle, shank, tactical pen, etc. When assuming this stance, drop your head down and keep your neck and throat behind both of your arms at all times. This diminishes target size and reduces the likelihood of a quick kill slash or stab to either your neck or subclavian artery.

Deeply crouch your body, with your shoulders and stomach sunk inward. This unusual posture brings your chest and internal organs away from dangerous puncture wounds. Both of your arms are held up, with your hands, forearms, and elbows close to your body to diminish target opportunities.

A knife fight should always be avoided at all costs. It is a desperate situation that should only be undertaken when all other means of avoiding the situation have been thoroughly exhausted. Always attempt to escape or run from a knife fight.

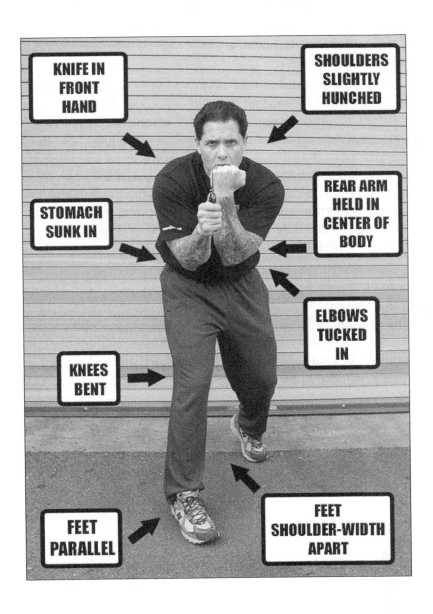

KNIFE IN FRONT HAND

SHOULDERS SLIGHTLY HUNCHED

STOMACH SUNK IN

REAR ARM HELD IN CENTER OF BODY

ELBOWS TUCKED IN

KNEES BENT

FEET PARALLEL

FEET SHOULDER-WIDTH APART

BLUDGEON DEFENSE STANCE

When unarmed and faced with a bludgeon (baseball bat, heavy club, 2X4, etc.) attack, the bludgeon defense stance is your safest bet.

It's also important to first determine your assailant's intent before assuming a bludgeon defense stance. It's critical to make an accurate threat assessment when confronted by a bludgeon-wielding assailant. Use split-second judgment to determine exactly what your adversary wants to accomplish. Some assailants might not want to harm you if they can avoid it. Others may be dead set on smashing your skull to pieces. If you have determined that your assailant plans to harm you, you must immediately assume this stance and resort to aggressive disarming techniques.

To assume this stance, keep your body angled approximately 45-degrees from the attacker with both of your arms raised to the sides of your head. Keep your torso slightly crouched with your arms and elbows close to your body. As with all the combat stances, keep your knees slightly bent and flexible with your feet shoulder-width apart, and your weight equally distributed on each leg.

One of the fundamental principles of bludgeon defense is familiarity. Take the time to familiarize yourself with as many types of bludgeons as possible. Learn the different types of grips, chamber positions, weights, and materials.

RANGE PROFICIENCY

A street fight is unfair and unpredictable. It can occur anytime and anywhere. So, if you want to win a fight, then you'd better be *range proficient*. Range proficiency is the skill and ability to defend and fight your adversary in all three distances of unarmed combat (kicking range, punching range, grappling range). Before addressing each range of combat, let's first take a look at the Neutral Zone.

The Neutral Zone

In unarmed combat, the neutral zone is not a range of combative engagement. It is the distance at which neither you or your opponent can physically strike one another with your limbs. From a defensive perspective, the neutral zone serves a strategic purpose by enhancing your defensive reaction time in the event that your opponent attacks you first. If the opponent is a grappler and elects to rush you from this distance, you will have sufficient reaction time to evade his attack. Moreover, if your objective is to effectively initiate a preemptive strike you must be standing in one of the three combat ranges, preferably punching or grappling range.

Kicking Range

The furthest distance of unarmed combat is kicking range. At this distance you are usually too far away to strike with your hands, so you would use your legs to strike your opponent. Kicking range tools can be safe, economical and powerful if they are delivered to targets below the opponent's waist.

 *If you're going to execute kicking techniques in a fight, always employ low-line kicks to targets below the assailant's waist. They are efficient, effective, deceptive, non telegraphic, and relatively safe.*

Punching Range

Punching range is the mid-range of unarmed combat. At this distance, you are close enough to the enemy to strike him with your hands and fists. Punching range tools are quick, efficient and effective and they are the foundation of your compound attack arsenal. Unlike the kicking range, you can effectively deliver a flurry of full-speed blows in the punching range. Most importantly, compared to the grappling range, the punching range requires only moderate bodily commitment.

Since punching range is the most tactically advantageous range of unarmed combat, your objective is to maintain this distance while delivering an overwhelming compound attack.

Grappling Range

The third and closest range of unarmed combat is grappling range. At this distance, you are too close to your opponent to kick or execute some hand strikes, so you would use close-quarter tools and techniques to neutralize your adversary. Bear in mind that grappling range is the most important distance of combat when defending against a grappler. Here you will learn to stop him dead in his tracks!

Moreover, grappling range is divided into two different planes, vertical and horizontal. In the vertical plane (also know as the clinch), you would deliver impact techniques, some of which include: elbow and knee strikes, head butts, gouging and crushing tactics, and biting and tearing techniques. In the horizontal plane, you are ground fighting with your enemy and can deliver all of the previously mentioned techniques, including various submission holds, locks, and chokes.

Understanding the Clinch

Now that you're aware of the various ranges of unarmed combat, you need to understand the defensive implications of the "clinch." First, clinching occurs in grappling range and it's the process of strategically locking up with your opponent while the two of you are standing.

Clinching should be employed off your initial defensive response (i.e., block, parry, slip, etc). For example, your adversary attacks you first with a hay maker, you block accordingly and move into a clinch. Once in the clinch you counter the opponent with a series of head butts, knee strikes and elbows. By strategically clinching, you negate your opponent's ability to maintain his offensive flow. The objective is to bypass his assault and reestablish offensive control.

The bottom line is if you are truly interested in "real world" self-defense skills, you must know how to fight in the clinch and ultimately control it. Remember that the clinch is the last range or phase of combat before the fight goes to the ground. So if you don't use this golden opportunity to neutralize your adversary, you can bet that the both of you are going to the ground. And the ground is one of the worst places to be when engaged in a street fight.

Interestingly enough, most street fights invariably end up with the two combatants locked up in a temporary clinch. Very seldom is it the result of strategic planning, more often it's the physical residual of two forces fueled by adrenaline, colliding into one another. Whatever its cause, the clinch is a very real element of combat that must be mastered if you are to defeat your adversary.

How to Control the Clinch

The most important aspect of controlling the clinch is using the proper gripping technique. While there are numerous combat systems that teach a wide variety of clinch positions, there is only one that really matters. I refer to it as the "inside position".

To assume the strategic inside position, start by placing both of your hands on the opponent's neck, clamp down hard and be certain that your hands overlap each other. Tuck your elbows in to protect against body shots. This type of neck hold is essential, if you control the opponent's head, you will ultimately control his body. Don't just pull your opponent with your arms; remember to use your entire body. Also, make certain that both of your forearms run over his collarbone. This arm positioning will throw your opponent off balance and set him up for a variety of close quarter strikes.

Avoid becoming too tense when clinching with your adversary. You want to be able to feel his weight, balance and energy shift when fighting. Keep in mind that you are safe in the clinch for a very brief period of time. You don't want to stay there long.

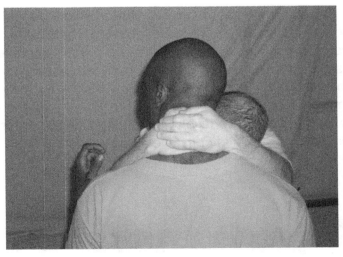

Here, a student shows the proper hand positioning for the clinch.

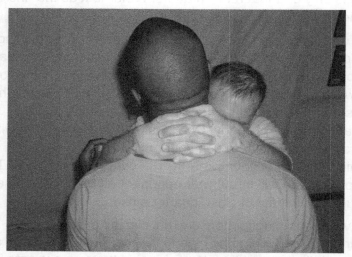

Avoid interlacing your fingers when clinching. In some cases your fingers can break.

Fighting in the Clinch

Once you have established the inside position, it's time to attack your adversary as quickly as possible. Head butts, knee strikes, elbow strikes, eye raking and eye gouges, and biting tactics should be employed. It is important that you are able to see the various windows of opportunity within the explosive dynamics of the fight. Your objective is to attack your enemy with explosive and powerful blows. You want to disturb his balance and prevent him from leveraging you into a throw or takedown.

Clinching is used for both offensive and defensive purposes. For defense, clinching should be employed immediately after you have performed a specific defensive technique such as a block, parry, stiff-arm jam, webbing technique, etc.

228

The head butt is just one of the weapons you can deliver in the clinch.

Raking the opponent's eyes when locked up in the clinch can be very effective.

229

Elbows strikes also work well in the clinch. Notice how Franco (right) uses his left hand to maintain control of his opponent's head.

MOBILITY

A proficient self-defense technician must be able to move swiftly. He must be mobile. Mobility is defined as the ability to move the body quickly and economically, and this can be accomplished through basic footwork. Safe footwork requires quick economical steps performed on the balls of the feet, while relaxed and balanced.

The Basics of Footwork

Basic footwork can be used for both offensive and defensive purposes, and it is structured around four general directions: advancing, retreating, sidestepping right and sidestepping left.

Moving forward (advancing) - From your fighting stance, first move your front foot forward (approximately 24 inches) and then move your rear foot an equal distance.

Moving backward (retreating) - From your fighting stance, first move your rear foot backward (approximately 24 inches) and then move your front foot an equal distance.

Moving right (sidestepping right) - From a fighting stance, first move your right foot to the right (approximately 24 inches) and then move your left foot an equal distance.

Moving left (sidestepping left) - From a fighting stance, first move your left foot to the left (approximately 24 inches) and then move your left foot an equal distance. Note: Practice these four movements everyday in front of a full-length mirror until your footwork is quick, balanced, and natural.

TO ADVANCE: From the starting position, first move your front foot forward (approximately 24 inches) and then move your rear foot an equal distance.

TO RETREAT: From your fighting stance, first move your rear foot backward (approximately 24 inches) and then move your front foot an equal distance.

MOVING RIGHT (sidestepping right): From a fighting stance, first move your right foot to the right (approximately 24 inches), and then move your left foot an equal distance.

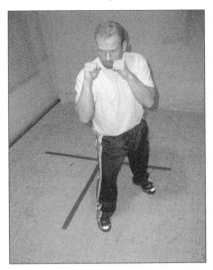 

MOVING LEFT (sidestepping left): From a fighting stance, first move your left foot to the left (approximately 24 inches) and then move your left foot an equal distance.

 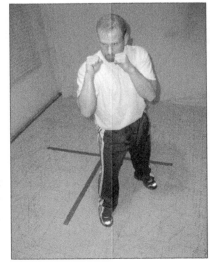

ADVANCED FOOTWORK

Once you have mastered basic footwork, you can then incorporate strategic circling to your repertoire of skills. Strategic circling is an advanced form of footwork where the warrior uses his lead leg as a pivot point.

This advanced footwork can be used defensively to evade an overwhelming assault or offensively to strike the enemy from various strategic angles. Strategic circling can be performed from either a right or left stance.

Circling right (from a right stance) - From a right lead stance, step 8 to 12 inches to the right with your right foot, use your right leg as a pivot point and wheel your entire rear leg to the right until the correct stance and positioning is acquired. Remember to keep both of your hands up.

Circling left (from a left stance) - From a left lead stance, step 8 to 12 inches to the left with your left foot, use your left leg as a pivot point and wheel your entire rear leg to the left until the correct stance and positioning is acquired.

No form of combat (armed or unarmed) is ever going to be a static encounter. There is always going to be some type of movement. Be prepared for it!

BLOCKING TECHNIQUES

Blocking techniques are defensive tools designed to intercept the assailant's attack by placing a non-vital limb (usually your arm) between the opponent's strike and his intended target.

There are four blocks that you need to be proficient with. They include: high blocks, mid blocks, low blocks and elbow blocks. To maximize the execution of your hand blocks, remember to always keep your hands open. Let's begin with the high block.

High Blocks

The high block is used to defend against overhead blows. To execute the lead high block, simply raise your lead arm up and extend your forearm out and above your head. Be careful not to position your arm where your head is exposed. Make certain that your hand is open and not clenched. This will increase the surface area of your block and provide a quick counterattack. The mechanics for the lead high block are the same for the rear high block. Raise your rear arm up and extend your forearm out and above your head.

Mid Blocks

The mid block is specifically used to defend against circular blows to your head or upper torso. To perform the block, raise either your right or left arm up at approximately 90 degrees while simultaneously pronating it into the direction of the strike. Make contact with the belly of your forearm at the assailant's wrist or forearm. This movement will provide maximum structural integrity for the blocking tool. Make certain that your hand is held open to increase the surface area of your block.

When performing the mid block, be certain to time the rotation of your arm with the attack. Don't forget that the mid block has both height (up and down) and a width (in and out) fluctuations that are relative to the characteristics of the assailant's blow. Remember, once you deliver the block, immediately counter.

Since most people are right handed, the most common blocks used in unarmed combat will be the left mid and high blocks.

236

Low Blocks

The low-block is used to defend against powerful linear shots to your midsection. To execute the lead low-block, drop your lead arm so your forearm is parallel to the ground and make certain that your fingers are pointing up to protect against jamming or breaks.

With the low-block, contact is made with the belly of the forearm and not the palm. The mechanics are the same for the rear low-block. Simply drop your rear arm down to meet the assailant's strike.

While low blocks are infrequently used, they're still an important component of your defensive system. Don't neglect them.

Elbow Blocks

The elbow block is used to stop circular blows to your midsection, like uppercuts, shovel hooks and hook kicks.

To execute the elbow block, drop your elbow down and simultaneously twist your body toward your centerline. Make certain to keep your elbow perpendicular to the floor and keep your hands relaxed and close to your chest. The elbow block can be used on both right and left sides.

CAUTION: Elbow blocks should only be used when you're absolutely certain your adversary isn't armed with a knife or edged weapon. If you can't clearly see his hands, avoid using them.

PARRYING TECHNIQUES

The parry is a quick forceful slap that picks off and redirects your assailant's linear attack (i.e., jabs, lead straights, and rear crosses, even linear knife stabs). There are two general types of parries for street fighting: horizontal and vertical. Both can be executed from the right and left hands.

Horizontal Parry

To properly execute a horizontal parry perform the following: From a stance move your lead hand horizontally across your body (centerline) to deflect and redirect the assailant's punch. Immediately return to your guard position. Make certain to make contact with the palm of your hand. With sufficient training, you can effectively incorporate the horizontal parry with your slipping maneuvers.

CAUTION: Don't parry a punch with your fingers. The fingers provide no structural integrity, and they can easily be jammed or broken.

Vertical Parry

To properly execute a vertical parry perform the following: From a stance move your lead hand vertically down your body (centerline) to deflect and redirect the assailant's punch. Immediately return to your guard position. Be certain to keep your fingers tight and compact while making contact with the palm of your hand.

Vertical parries aren't just for deflecting linear punches. In some circumstances, they can also be used against linear kicks directed to your waist and torso region.

EVASION TECHNIQUES

Evading skills are simply defensive maneuvers designed to strategically move you away from your assailant's attack. There are many variations of evasion. One of the most common is slipping.

Slipping

Slipping is a quick defensive maneuver that permits you to avoid an assailant's linear blow (jab, lead straight, rear cross, and palm heel) without stepping out of range. Safe and effective slipping requires precise timing and is accomplished by quickly snapping the head and upper torso sideways (right or left) to avoid the oncoming blow.

One of the greatest advantages to slipping is that it frees your hands so that you can simultaneous counter your attacker.

CHAPTER SEVEN
Outnumbered

MULTIPLE ATTACKER DEFENSE

Because many street punks characteristically attack in groups, it's important to learn how to defend against multiple attackers. Since power lies in their numbers, the odds are heavily stacked against you. Nevertheless, you can survive this type of threat by applying the knowledge and skill featured in this section.

To begin, there are two different types of multiple attacker scenarios you need to be aware of, and they include:

The Ambush - The practitioner is caught off guard and ambushed by his attackers. One of the best defenses for this type of attack is developing a strong sense of situational awareness.

The Set-Up - The practitioner is first approached by the attackers and set-up for the attack. Usually there is some brief dialogue between the attackers and the victim. The set-up differs from the ambush because it offers you greater control of the situation. In fact, your survivability improves significantly because you have more options, tactics, techniques, and strategies at your disposal.

TRY TO ESCAPE

When faced with multiple attackers, quickly scan your environment and look for any possible escape routes. Look for windows, doors, fire escapes, staircases, fences, escalators, or any other avenue that will allow you to flee quickly and safely from this situation. If the opportunity presents itself for you to run and escape safely, take it. Don't let your ego get in the way. *WARNING: Make sure that your version of an escape route doesn't lead you into a worse situation.*

A *barrier* is any object that obstructs the attacker's path of attack. At the very least, barriers give you distance and some precious time, and they may give you some safety - at least temporarily. A barrier must have the structural integrity to perform the particular function you have assigned it.

LOOK FOR MAKESHIFT WEAPONS

If you can't escape the situation, look for any possible *makeshift weapons* that can drastically turn the odds in your favor. Broken bottles, sticks, pipes, crowbars, and shards of broken glass are excellent equalizers that can quickly and effectively neutralize your assailants. However, make certain that you are proficient with these different types of weapons before attempting to use them against your attackers. Otherwise, they may use them against you and make matters worse.

Makeshift weapons can be broken down into the following (4) four types: a) cutting, b) shielding, c) distracting, and d) striking.

Cutting makeshift weapons are objects or implements used to stab or slash your assailant. Examples include: utility knives, forks, ice pick, screwdriver, broken glass, straight razor, pen, pencil, large nail, ice scraper, fire poker, crow bar, car keys, pitch fork, shovel, hack saw, knitting needle, spike, hatchet, meat hook, scissors, etc.

Shielding makeshift weapons are objects used to shield yourself from attack. Examples of shielding makeshift weapons include the following: briefcases, trash-can lids, bicycles, thick sofa cushions, backpacks, barstools, lawn chairs, drawers, cafeteria trays, suitcases, thick pillows, leather jackets/coats, sleeping bags, motorcycle helmets, small end tables, hubcaps, etc. Once again, be certain that your makeshift weapon has the structural integrity to get the job done effectively.

Distracting makeshift weapons are objects that can be thrown into your assailant's face, torso, or legs to temporarily distract him. Generally distracting makeshift weapons are thrown into your assailant's face. Some examples include the following: sunglasses, magazines, car keys, wallets, ashtrays, books, salt shakers, alarm clocks, coins, bottles, bars of soap, shoes, dirt, sand, gravel, rocks, videotapes, small figurines, cassette tapes, watering can, hot liquids, paperweights, pesticide sprays, and oven cleaner spray.

Striking makeshift weapons are objects used to strike the assailant. Examples of striking makeshift weapons include sticks, bricks, crowbars, baseball bats, shovels, golf clubs, lamps, books, light chair, pool cues, pipes, heavy flashlights, hammers, binoculars, glass bottles, beer mugs, tool boxes, briefcases, car doors, canes, walking sticks, automobile, light dumbbells, 2 x 4s, etc.

Makeshift Weapon Targets

Knowledge of the various makeshift weapons isn't enough. You must have a foundational understanding of the anatomical targets that are vulnerable to each of the three makeshift weapon classifications.

Cutting weapons targets include the enemy's ear cavities, eye sockets, temples, base of skull, cervical vertebrae, jugular vein, underside of the chin, carotid artery, subclavian, heart, lungs, wrists, back of knees, Achilles tendons, brachial arteries, radial arteries, third and fourth rib regions, solar plexus, groin, and femoral arteries.

Distracting weapons targets include the enemy's face and eyes, groin, and legs.

Striking weapon targets include the enemy's head, throat, back of neck, clavicle, lower back, elbows, hands and forearms, ribs, thighs, and knees.

KEEP MOVING

Whenever faced with multiple attackers, always keep moving. Mobility makes you a difficult target to hit and prevents your assailants from surrounding you. Mobility also enhances the power of your blows and makes your attackers misjudge your range. Most importantly, mobility may help you locate an open area in which to safely escape.

DON'T GET SURROUNDED

Never, ever let yourself be surrounded by your attackers. It is impossible to defend yourself in every possible direction all at once. Mobility can help prevent you from being trapped. Constantly angle your body so there is always one assailant between you and the rest of them. Take advantage of your environment by trying to maneuver yourself in strategic positions, such as between parked cars or doorways. This prevents them from utilizing their full strength and can permit you to fight them one at a time.

Some instructors advise you to keep your back to the wall to prevent being surrounded. I strongly disagree with this because it inhibits your mobility and limits the body mechanics of your fighting techniques. The wall will also provide a possible striking surface for your assailant to smash your head or body.

DETERMINE WHO IS THE IMMEDIATE THREAT

When unarmed and faced with multiple attackers, you must divide them and attack the assailant who presents the most immediate threat to you. Usually the armed assailant is your most immediate threat. If none of the attackers are armed with a weapon, then go for the one closest to you. If more than one attacker is of equal distance from you, then the assailant who is blocking your escape route is the most immediate threat.

Finally, if more than one assailant is blocking your escape route, go for leader or *alpha* of the group. He's the ringleader who fuels the "spirit of the group" which motivates the others to attack. Also, he's often the one with the biggest mouth.

ATTACK THE IMMEDIATE THREAT

Once you've determined which assailant is the greatest threat, attack him immediately. Quickly move to the flank of the assailant and attack with a barrage of swift blows. Your tactical objective is to injure him as quickly and as efficiently as possible. Remember to strike first, strike fast, strike with authority, and keep the pressure on.

Because of the extreme threat and danger posed by multiple attackers, <u>it's imperative that you make an example of your first assailant</u>. Attack him with extreme prejudice. For example, if the other assailants see their partner violently choking from a brutal throat strike, it might kill their spirit to continue their assault on you.

ATTACK THE EYES OR THROAT

Assuming range isn't an issue, the two primary anatomical targets to strike in a multiple attacker situation are the *eyes* and *throat*. This is not to say that other targets don't matter – they certainly do! However, you should focus your strikes at the eyes and throat because they can instantly disable your attackers. *Warning! Always be certain your self-defense actions are legally and morally justified in the eyes of the law!*

EMPLOY THE ASSEMBLY LINE PRINCIPLE

When attacking the immediate threat, try to maneuver yourself so a straight line is created between you and all of the attackers. I call this the *assembly line principle* because it temporarily forces assailant number one to be a natural barrier between you and the other attackers. Once again, this will only buy you a couple of seconds, but a few precious seconds can make all the difference between life and death in the streets.

APPLY THE HUMAN SHIELD PRINCIPLE.

Once you've injured the first attacker, use him as an obstacle or *human shield* to the help prevent the other attackers from reaching or attacking you. For example, try pushing or swinging him into the other attackers. This will momentarily slow down the other assailants and give you a few seconds to either escape or attack again.

Here, the author demonstrates the human shield principle.

While kicking techniques might buy you some time by temporarily keeping multiple assailants at bay, you'll need to resort to aggressive punching range techniques, like eye and throat strikes.

251

CHAPTER EIGHT
Breaching The Stronghold

HOME DEFENSE

DEALING WITH A HOME INVASION

The serious martial artist thinks nothing of spending countless hours conditioning and preparing for a possible assault on the street. However, very few of these practitioners are adequately prepared to handle an intruder in their home. Richard Ramirez, the infamous "Night Stalker" who terrorized Los Angeles residents for nearly a year before being caught and convicted, was notorious for his ability to surreptitiously enter victims' homes, rob them, and in many cases kill or rape family members before leaving.

The Ramirez case is just one of many similar occurrences going on in American homes each night across the country. But the unfortunate fact is, criminal intrusion is a subject seldom addressed in the martial arts studio. Yet, according to law enforcement statistics, there is a strong possibility such an occurrence can happen to you and your family.

Ask yourself these important questions: Do you have a tactical plan should some scumbag invade your home? Do you have the knowledge and expertise to keep both you and your family out of harm's way? Do you own a firearm, and are you trained to use it in this type of situation? Do you have a designated safe room? If you answered "no" to any of these questions, you and your loved ones may be at great risk. The Following are several suggestions to help you prepare for an intruder in your home.

Plan Ahead

Design a tactical plan for you and your family. Begin by drawing a detailed diagram of your home, then discuss your safety options and the various strategies you can employ if a criminal breaks into your house. Make certain all of your family members are familiar with the layout of your home. Including all entrances, escape routes, and possible ambush zones. Discuss what types of makeshift weapons are located throughout the house, and make certain everyone knows how to use them correctly.

You will also need a designated "safe room" where family members can escape from the intruder and wait for the police to arrive. Most people choose a particular bedroom in their house. Be certain there is a charged cellphone in the safe room so you can contact an emergency dispatcher during a threatening encounter.

If you have a security system in your home, make certain everyone is familiar with its operation and limitations. Don't rely, however, on the security system to alert you to an intruder. A seasoned criminal can break into any home undetected. Even if an alarm warns you of danger, it does not eliminate the threat. Remember, you and only you are responsible for your own safety and survival.

Alert the Cops

If you think there is an intruder in your home, call the police immediately—even if you aren't absolutely certain. It is better to be safe than sorry. In most cities, you simply need to dial 911 to speak to an emergency dispatcher; Remain calm., collect your thoughts, and tell the dispatcher the following information: your name and address; the type of crime being committed; the approximate location of the intruder(s); the intruder's general description, if possible; the exact location of you and your family members; whether anyone is injured; and if you (or the intruder) are armed with a firearm or other weapon.

Stay in Your Safe Room

Remain in the safe room until the police arrive; Keep the door of the room locked and have everyone stay away from the entrance. If possible, find cover behind a protective barrier (a bed, perhaps). If you do own a firearm, keep it pointed at the door. Stay focused and alert. Under no circumstances should you leave the safe room and search the house for the intruder. This is extremely dangerous and should be left to the police.

If the intruder attempts to enter the safe room, tell him that you have called the police, that they are on their way, and that you are armed with a gun. If the intruder still attempts to force his way in, and if he presents a deadly threat to you or your family, you have every right to shoot him.

Holding an Intruder at Gunpoint

If you somehow manage to capture and hold the criminal intruder at gunpoint, be sure to keep him at a safe distance and in an awkward position. Make sure that both of his hands are always in clear view. If possible, order the intruder to do the following:

1. Make him turn and face away from you so he can't see what you're doing.

2. Tell him to slowly raise his hands straight over his head. Be certain you can see his fingertips.

3. Have him slowly drop to his knees, without using his hands.

4. Once on his knees, have him cross one leg over the other.

5. Next, have him lie on his stomach with his arms at his sides.

6. Tell him to place his hands flat on the floor with his palms facing up.

Under no circumstances should you allow him to get within grabbing distance of your firearm. And do not search him for any weapons. Simply keep him in this awkward position until the police arrive.

Don't engage in any conversation with the intruder. Bark out your orders firmly and confidently; let him know you mean business. Keep your finger on the trigger and aim the gun at the center of his body. Don't ever take your eyes off him, and be aware that he might have an accomplice in the house.

Stay with the intruder until the police arrive, but be careful about greeting the authorities with a gun (or any weapon) in your hand. The first officers on the scene have no way of knowing who is the homeowner and who is the criminal. Until they sort things out, keep any weapons out of sight.

Save Any Evidence

Do not move, clean or discard anything until the police arrive and have made a full report of the incident. You don't want to destroy any physical evidence the intruder might have left behind, including fingerprints. Avoid touching anything he might have touched. Broken windows, forced locks, overturned furniture, blood, hair, dirt, mud, etc., might reveal important information about the intruder.

If a member of your family was raped by the intruder, it is imperative that you do not change your clothes, comb your hair, shower, bathe, or douche before being examined by a physician. As repulsive as it may seem, it is essential to temporarily stay the way you are if you want to assist in the conviction of the attacker. Semen, hair and other samples can serve as damaging evidence against your assailant in court.

Post-Traumatic Syndrome

Whether you are the victor or the victim of a violent confrontation with an intruder, the incident will likely change you in some way. The emotional trauma of violence can either strengthen or destroy you. You may experience a variety of debilitating conditions, including denial, shock, fear, anger and depression. You may also experience eating and sleeping disorders, societal withdrawal and paranoia.

Even if you justifiably crippled or killed the intruder you may experience emotional residuals; Killing another human being, even in the act of self-defense. It isn't easy for some people to live with and can cause insomnia, nightmares, depression, guilt, lack of concentration and anxiety.

Criminal Awareness

You and your family should have a general understanding of criminals' motivations, mentalities, methods and capabilities to perpetrate violent acts. By staying abreast of criminal activity through the media, official crime reports, and other sources, you can gain insight into the types and trends of violent crime. When analyzing other home invasions you have read about, ask yourself the following questions:

- Who was the victim, and who was the intruder?
- What happened during the intrusion?
- Where did the intrusion take place?

259

- When was the intrusion committed?
- Why did the intrusion occur?
- Why that perpetrator?
- Why that house?
- And, finally, how did the criminal break in?

Answer these questions as thoroughly as you can, and you will learn a great deal about home invasions. You will also be obtaining an invaluable education that can protect both you and your family.

Other Good Tips and Strategies

The Following are some other important tips and strategies you can incorporate into your home safety plan. These pointers are not intended to limit your life-style; they are merely presented to help make you and your family less vulnerable to an intruder. Take whatever works for you.

- Always keep a flashlight close to your bed.
- Keep doors and windows locked at all times.
- When sleeping, keep your bedroom door locked to help delay criminal entry.
- Never leave your garage door open or unlocked.
- Never enter your home if it shows signs of entry.
- Leave interior and exterior lights on all night.
- Do not hide spare keys outside your home.
- Do not rely on watchdogs. They may not hear the intruder, and they can be - and have been - poisoned by criminals.
- Know your neighbors. Know who belongs in your neighborhood and who doesn't.
- Form and/or join a neighborhood watch program.
- Put dead bolts, each with a minimum one-inch throw, on

all doors. Do not use security chains on your doors. They can be easily broken.

• Keep trees and shrubbery around windows and doors well trimmed.

• Secure all sliding glass doors with bar braces and/or special locks.

• Install a wide-angle peephole in your front door.

• Install new locks when moving into a house or apartment.

• Be suspicious of all unanticipated delivery persons.

• Never give your keys to service people, such as carpenters, painters, repairmen, etc.

• To help the police identify your home quickly, make certain your address is clearly visible from the street.

• Don't leave messages on your front door; they tell criminals that you are not home.

• Don't put your name and address on your key rings.

CHAPTER NINE
The Devil In The Details

STREET SURVIVAL TIPS

These rules and guidelines will help you avoid becoming a victim. They are not intended to limit your life-style, but to help make what you do a lot safer. Remember, no matter how extreme the precautionary measures are, you may still be confronted with a dangerous situation.

AUTOMOTIVE SAFETY

• Familiarize yourself with your usual travel routes. Be aware of detours or construction sites and avoid traveling deserted roads.

• Consider carrying a "call police" banner in your car, in case your car breaks down on the side of the road.

• Be particularly alert at red lights, stop signs, and gas stations.

• When approaching your car, always look under and inside the vehicle before you get too close to it, and then enter it.

• Know how to defend yourself if attacked in your car.

• If your car breaks down, raise the hood and stay inside with the doors locked. If a motorist approaches you, slightly roll down the window and ask him or her to call for assistance.

• Never accept a ride from a stranger.

• Never leave your driver's license, car registration, or operator's manual in your car.

• If your own a Jeep or convertible, be alert when driving with the top down at night.

• When parking your car in a mall, consider leaving a man's hat or pipe on the passenger seat. It makes it look like a male companion is with you.

• Always report any suspicious people loitering in store parking lots.

• When approaching intersections or stoplights, always keep your car in gear and be prepared to drive away immediately.

•Never pull into a parking space next to anyone loitering or sitting in a parked car, and never get out of your car if there is a suspicious person present.

• Keep your car in good running condition. Routinely check the oil, hoses, water, tires, and battery. Never run out of gas. There is no excuse for putting yourself in that situation.

• If another motorist drives aggressively, cuts you off, tails you too closely, etc., Don't retaliate.

• Never drive under the influence of drugs or alcohol.

• Learn how to change a flat tire. Practice it in the safety of your driveway or home before confronting the real thing on the road.

• Keep in mind that 80 percent of all terrorist attacks take place in or near a vehicle. Car bombs have been used in approximately 67 percent of such attacks.

• Never follow any other vehicle too closely.

• Do not put controversial or offensive bumper stickers, or other signs on your car.

• Keep the following items in your car: gas can, jumper cables, a white rag, cellphone changer, credit card, fresh drinking water, maps, first-aid kit, flashlight, flares, and a spare tire and jack.

• Never leave your child alone in your car.

• Be particularly alert when parking in underground garages.

• If a criminal is shooting at you while you're driving your car. Drop down low, sound the horn, and escape immediately.

• When parking your car, turn your wheels sharply to the right or left. This makes it difficult for car thieves to tow your car away.

• In the event of an emergency, be familiar with various safe havens along your daily travel routes.

• Never drive home if you think you are being followed. Instead drive to the nearest police or fire station and draw attention by sounding the horn.

• When leaving your car in a shopping center or mall. always make a mental note where you parked so you don't waste time looking for your car.

• When driving in the city or populated areas, keep your windows rolled up. If you don't have air conditioning, keep the windows cracked slightly.

• Avoid using personalized license plates. This form of vanity, like others, can get you into trouble by attracting bad elements and making it easier for them to identify and follow your vehicle.

• Always approach your car with your key in hand, ready to unlock the door without delay.

• Do not stop to assist motorists beside the road—no matter what! If someone attempts to flag you down, don't stop.

• Never make insulting gestures to other motorists. If someone insults you, ignore it.

• Never leave valuables in your car.

• If your car is broken into, do not touch a thing; contact the police immediately.

• Try to pick busy streets for your travel. When walking on isolated streets, stay away from alleys, doorways, and parked vans or automobiles.

• When driving to automated teller machines, survey the surroundings for suspicious people. Anyone you don't know should be viewed with a healthy suspicion.

• Try to park your car in highly visible, well-lighted, populated areas.

• When driving, check your side- and rear-view mirrors to see if you are being followed. If unsure, take a diversionary route to make sure you're not.

• If lost, don't ask strangers for directions. Go into a busy store or hotel or approach a police officer. Hospitals and fire stations are also good places to ask for directions.

• If your car breaks down, raise the hood, tie a handkerchief to the door handle, and stay in your car with the doors locked until police assistance arrives.

• When stopped in traffic, stay far enough behind the car in front of you to safely pull around it and drive away. This extra space will permit a quick escape if it becomes necessary.

• Never pick up hitchhikers.

• When you enter your car, lock the doors before you fasten your seat belt.

• Keep you car doors locked at all times, even when parked at home.

STREET SAFETY

• Always turn wide corners. Do not go around corners within 5 feet of a wall, building, shrubbery, etc.

• Do not walk down the street looking lost, fatigued, uncertain, or preoccupied. Assertive body language is essential. Keep your head up and walk with confidence and purpose, even if you are lost.

• Learn to use store windows and other reflecting sources to note suspicious activity behind you.

• Familiarize yourself with ambush zones and avoid them whenever possible.

- When walking in the streets, avoid high-crime areas.
- Assume that violence can, and very well may, occur anywhere.
- Constantly scan your environment, thoroughly and quickly noting potential problems.
- When entering a dark environment, allow a few seconds for your eyes to adjust before moving on.
- When walking down the street, if something doesn't feel right, listen to your instincts and get the heck out of there.
- If a car approaches you while you are walking down the street and you are harassed by the drivers, yell and run in the opposite direction.
- Never turn your back on a potential aggressor unless he is so far away he can't reach you before you get to safety.
- Do not take shortcuts through alleys, parking lots. tunnels, parks, construction sites, or abandoned buildings.
- Avoid poorly lit stairwells and bus stops.
- Don't argue with anyone, give offensive gestures, or engage in eye wars.
- Don't display money or jewelry.
- Don't carry large amount of cash.
- Avoid walking, hiking, or jogging alone. Try to get a friend or family member to go with you.
- Avoid carrying a lot of packages at once; this can make you an easy target. Try to keep at least one hand free at all times.
- Wear clothes and shoes that facilitate quick and free movement. Try to wear sneakers or shoes with low heels. If you are wearing high heels and are being chased, kick them off and run barefoot.

• Do not be in denial about how dangerous and violent the streets can be.

• Don't sleep on public transportation and try not to use it if fatigued or intoxicated.

• Know your bus schedule to avoid long waits at the bus stop.

• When traveling on the subway, stay alert at all times.

• When exiting a bus, watch who is getting off with you and who is waiting at the stop,

• Vary your travel routes. Constant patterns allow assailants to monitor your behavior, note the regularity of your schedule, and pick an opportune time for attack.

• When getting money at machines or teller windows, put it away before leaving.

• If a physical confrontation with an assailant seems inevitable, then strike first, fast, repeatedly, and then escape.

• Do not carry more credit cards than you plan to use.

• Destroy all credit card carbon copies before leaving an establishment.

• Plan your hiking, jogging, and walking routes. Do not travel through dangerous areas containing a high number of high-risk ambush zones. If possible, let someone know what your route will be and how long you plan to be gone.

• Walk, run, or jog in the opposite direction of traffic.

• Avoid tunnel vision when exercising or doing anything for that matter. Stay aware and alert.

• Be wary in public rest rooms.

• When entering a taxi, observe the driver's identification card and make sure it matches his face. If there isn't a picture ID card, get out immediately.

• If you think you are being followed when walking down a street, immediately cross the street at a 90-degree angle and observe the behavior of everyone else on the street. Remember, you can be followed or trailed from directions other that the one immediately behind you.

• When waiting for the elevator, stand approximately 6 feet away from the doors.

• Do not get on an elevator with a lone male stranger if you can avoid it. If you are about to exit an elevator and there is a suspicious person on the landing, do not exit the elevator. If you enter an elevator alone and a suspicious person joins you, get off immediately. If that's not possible, push a number of buttons for stops including the immediately available floor. If you are attacked on the elevator. push all the buttons. This will deny your attacker privacy.

• On public transportation sit in the aisle as close as possible to the driver. On subways, pick cars as close to the operator's car as possible.

• Do not carry chemical sprays, stun guns, knives, or guns unless you have been trained adequately in their use.

• Try to sit with your back to the wall in public places.

• Before entering convenience stores, banks, etc., take a quick look inside to make sure no trouble is going down.

• When walking on public streets, keep your purse close to your body with a firm grip and with the flap facing you.

• Know the escape routes in familiar buildings. In unfamiliar buildings, look around for fire exits, kitchen routes, etc.

• If you are ever confronted with an exhibitionist flasher, contact the police immediately.

• Try to stay in good shape.

• To avoid being pick pocketed, keep your wallet in your front pocket.

- Don't allow strangers to stop you on the street.
- Try to avoid streets where groups of teenagers congregate.
- When walking the streets at night, try to travel in pairs or groups.
- Never divulge personal information (name, age, home or work address, phone number) to any stranger.
- When shopping, never leave your valuables unattended in a fitting room. When grocery shopping, never leave your purse unattended in your cart.
- When visiting recreational facilities (beaches, parks, movie theaters, bars, etc.), avoid calling attention to yourself with loud or boisterous behavior.
- When making a purchase in a store, never recite your cellphone number to the store cashier. Instead, write it down.
- If you must attend the movies alone, avoid sitting in the last few rows.
- If you must run or exercise outdoors in the evening, wear reflective clothing and don't wear a Walkman.
- Do not try to reason with a potential assailant unless you are buying time to escape, signaling for help, or setting up a counterattack.
- If you are being attacked on the street, smash a store window to attract attention.
- If you are kidnapped or taken hostage, remain as calm as possible. Don't argue, question, or lecture your captors. Wait for a solid opportunity to escape and take it. Don't hesitate, but don't attempt escape prematurely.
- If you are kidnapped or taken hostage, prepare yourself for possible verbal and physical abuse, as well as lack of food, water, and sanitation.

CHILD SAFETY

• Instruct your children not to talk to strangers.

• Teach your children not to accept gifts from strangers.

• Do not allow your children to use recreational play areas unless they are supervised by responsible adults whom you know.

• When teaching street safety to your kids, emphasize caution, not fear.

• Teach your kids to routinely inform you of their whereabouts.

• Instruct your children that no one has the right to touch their bodies except the family physician.

• When grocery shopping, never leave your child unattended in your cart.

• When hiring a baby-sitter, get to know the person well and always check references.

• Teach your children not to keep secrets, especially from you.

• Always support your kids' decisions to refuse to hug or kiss a relative like "Uncle Steve" or "Aunt Dottie." This makes it easier for them to say "No" if a stranger wants to touch them.

• If your child is going door-to-door for a school project always accompany him or her and conduct business outside.

• Always try to accompany your children to public rest rooms. If that is not possible, then carefully monitor the length of time they are in there.

• Consider having your children's fingerprints taken and stored safely.

• If you suspect your child has been assaulted or sexually abused, contact the police immediately.

• Know where your children are at all times.

• Instruct your children not to eat candy or foodstuffs from strangers, especially on Halloween.

• For identification purposes, always have a recent photograph of your child.

• Make certain your children know their names, phone number, and address.

• Never write your child's name on his or her clothes, book bags, lunch box, etc.

HOME SAFETY

• Keep doors and windows locked at all times.

• When sleeping, keep your bedroom doors locked.

• Never invite strangers into your home, no matter who they say they are.

• Never leave your garage door open or unlocked.

• Never enter your home if it shows any signs of possible entry. Go to a neighbor's and call the police.

• In the evening, leave interior and exterior lights on all night. Vary the lights you choose to leave on inside the house.

• Do not hide spare keys anywhere outside your home.

• Do not open your door to strangers. If it's a law enforcement officer, ask to see identification. He or she will understand.

• Never keep large sums of money in your house.

• Don't rely solely on watchdogs. They can be, and have been, poisoned by intruders.

• To discourage burglars, keep your drapes, curtains, and blinds drawn in the evening.

• If you keep firearms in your home. Keep them in a burglar proof safe when you are away. Keep them away from children at all times. Be trained extensively in safe handling and self-defense procedures. Armed novices are dangerous to themselves and others.

• Report any voyeurs to the police immediately.

• Know your neighbors. Know who belongs in your neighborhood and who doesn't. Get to know your neighbors' cars.

• Form and/or join neighborhood watch programs.

• Do not rely on security chains on doors.

• Keep the trees and shrubbery around windows and doors well trimmed.

• Use only your initials and last names on mailboxes.

• Put dead bolts on all doors and make certain they all have a minimum 1-inch throw. Never rely on spring bolts. They can be jimmied very easily.

• If possible, avoid glass panel or hollow-wood exterior doors. A determined criminal will blast right through them.

• Make certain all exterior doors are solid with 1 3/4-inch hardwood.

• Install a wide-angle viewer in your front door.

• Don't rely solely on burglar alarms or electronic security systems. They can be disarmed. Further, they simply serve as a warning of danger. You must have a planned and effective response to the danger itself. Sit down with your family and design a few strategic plans to handle various home emergencies (e.g., burglary, fire. flood, etc.)

• If you live in an apartment building, avoid using the stairs.

• When moving into a new house or apartment, install new locks.

• Secure sliding glass exterior doors with bar braces.

- Make certain all window screens are properly latched,

- Be suspicious of all unanticipated delivery persons.

- Never give your keys to service people, i.e., carpenters, painters, repairmen, etc.

- Never leave ladders unchained outside your home, and never leave them up against the house.

- Avoid keeping your car keys and house keys on the same ring. Parking lot attendants can duplicate your house keys.

- If you live in an apartment building with an elevator, test the emergency button. If it stops the elevator, don't use it if you are in an elevator with a suspicious person or an attacker. You don't want to be stuck between floors with your assailant.

- Always keep a flashlight close to your bed or night stand.

- Never put your name and address on your key ring.

- Routinely check the locks on all the doors around your house.

- If ever you are attacked in your apartment hallway, avoid yelling "help!" Instead scream "fire!" Most tenants will rush out of their apartments.

- To help the police or fire department identify your home quickly, make certain your house number is clearly visible to the street.

- Don't leave messages on your front door: they tell burglars that you're not home.

- To make your home look occupied, keep the lawn sprinkler on when you leave the house.

- Keep your garage door closed and cover garage windows to keep burglars from looking in.

- If you ever confront a burglar in your home, stay calm. Do not try to stop him. If possible, try to escape to safety.

• If you have a safe in your home, avoid hiding your keys or combination number in obvious places.

• Write down the license number of suspicious vehicles that drive through your neighborhood.

• To discourage prowlers, consider installing floodlights in your backyard.

WORKPLACE SAFETY

• When work is over, try to encourage your co-workers to leave together.

• Be aware of the people who work in your office or building.

• Always lock your wallet or purse in your drawer.

• Avoid having your name or title displayed at your company parking lot.

• Avoid working late in the office.

• If you are going to work late, try to do it with another employee.

• If you notice any suspicious people in your building or office, notify security or police.

• Know where all the various fire escapes are located in your building.

• Avoid taking the stairs in your building.

• Be particularly cautious in deserted rest rooms.

• If you are leaving work in the evening, ask the security guard to escort you to your car.

• Ask your company's human resources division to arrange a self-defense seminar for all of the employees.

VACATION AND TRAVEL SAFETY

• Avoid political hot spots. Listen in advance to the news media for stories on places you plan to visit and learn about the political situation there. Even be careful of so-called stable democracies (consider the attacks that have taken place in England and Italy). No matter where your political views lie, you don't want to be an innocent victim. Call the State Department for information on countries you plan to visit.

• Try to travel light. Use hard shell luggage to avoid easy theft from soft travel bags.

• Avoid leaving your car in airport parking lots. Take a taxi or ask a friend for a lift.

• When on vacation, leave a car in the driveway and have the paper and mail stopped. The post office will hold your mail.

• When away, try to have your house appear to be occupied. Install timers on lights, TVs, and radios, and change the intervals. Also ask a friend or neighbor to keep an eye on things.

• Know the location and phone number of the U.S. Embassy and consular office in any foreign country you visit.

• Plan trips with reputable travel and touring agents. Don't look like a tourist and wander around alone if you can avoid it.

• If your plane is hijacked, remain calm and alert, keep your mouth shut, don't draw attention to yourself, and never volunteer to do anything. Above all, don't debate political or other issues. If your captors demand identification, surrender your passport immediately.

• When traveling abroad, avoid wearing ethnic or religious clothing. Try to blend with the local population and don't wear T-shirts or clothing sporting political slogans.

• If you work for the government, don't bring official documents onboard the plane. Pack them away. You don't want to be identified as an agent of the government. If you travel on a diplomatic passport, your agency will brief you accordingly.

• Try to book direct, secure-route flights to foreign countries. Stopover flights increase the likelihood of bomb emplacement or other terrorist activity.

• Avoid aisle seats on planes. They put you right next to where hijackers will be moving up and down the plane and possibly choosing hostages or victims. Instead, request window, exit, or rear seats.

• If you are on a hijacked plane that is stormed by a rescue team, dive for cover, stay down. and don't move until told to do so. If you must move, belly crawl while staying low to the ground.

• When traveling, don't tell strangers you are traveling alone.

• Make all reservations at reputable hotels. Be familiar with exits, entrances, and rest rooms.

• As soon as you arrive in another country, go to the authorities and try to find out where the dangerous areas are. Every city has them, and the police know where they are.

• Vary your travel routes and times, and always maintain a low profile.

• Avoid reading road maps in public places (restaurants, hotel lobbies, gas stations). You don't want strangers to know you are traveling.

• When in the airport, report any suspicious people or activities to security personnel.

APPENDIX
Code of Conduct

- Be loyal to family, friends and country.

- Be fearless in the face of danger.

- Carry yourself with dignity and grace.

- Be tenacious with all of your endeavors.

- Be decisive and stick to your convictions and beliefs.

- Don't genuflect or prostrate to another, ever.

- Have compassion for the weak or handicapped.

- Be self-confident at all times.

- Be accountable for all of your actions.

- Obey the law.

- Don't abuse your body with controlled substances.

- Admit when you are wrong.

- Be skeptical yet open-minded.

- Reject complacency.

- Never feel sorry for yourself.

- Never make the same mistake twice.

- Always speaks the truth.

- Don't be concerned what others may think of you.

- Never succumbs to the trappings of immediate gratification.

GLOSSARY

Many of the terms in this book may be strange to the first time reader. This is because most of the lexicon in this text are unique only to Contemporary Fighting Arts. What follows are some important terms often used in my CFA system.

A

Accuracy - The precise or exact projection of force. Accuracy is also defined as the ability to execute a combative movement with precision and exactness.

Action - A series of moving parts that permit a firearm to be loaded, unloaded and fired.

Adaptability - The ability to physically and psychologically adjust to new or different conditions or circumstances of combat.

Aerobic Exercise - "With air." Exercise that elevates the heart rate to a training level for a prolonged period of time, usually 30 minutes.

Affective Domain - This includes the attitudes, philosophies, ethics, values, discretionary use-of-force, and the spirit (killer instinct) required to use your combative tool or technique appropriately.

Affective Preparedness - Being emotionally and spiritually prepared for the demands and strains of combat.

Aggression - Hostile and injurious behavior directed toward a person.

Aggressive Hand Positioning - Placement of hands so as to imply aggressive or hostile intentions.

Aggressive Stance - (See Fighting Stance.)

Aggressor - One who commits an act of aggression.

Agility - An attribute of combat. One's ability to move his or

283

her body quickly and gracefully.

Amalgamation - A scientific process of uniting or merging.

Ambidextrous - The ability to perform with equal facility on both the right and left sides of the body.

Ambush - To lie in wait and attack by surprise.

Ambush Zones - Strategic locations (in everyday environments) from which assailants launch surprise attacks.

American Stick Strangle - A stick strangle used with a hammer grip.

Analysis and Integration - One of the five elements of CFA's mental component. This is the painstaking process of breaking down various elements, concepts, sciences, and disciplines into their atomic parts, and then methodically and strategically analyzing, experimenting, and drastically modifying the information so that it fulfills three combative requirements: efficiency, effectiveness and safety. Only then is it finally integrated into the CFA system.

Anatomical Handles - Various body parts (i.e., appendages, joints, and in some cases, organs) that can be grabbed, held, pulled or otherwise manipulated during a ground fight.

Anatomical Power Generators - Three points on the human body that help torque your body to generate impact power. Anatomical Power Generators include: (1) Feet; (2) Hips; (3) Shoulders.

Anatomical Striking Targets - The various anatomical body targets that can be struck and which are especially vulnerable to potential harm. They include: the eyes, temple, nose, chin, back of neck, front of neck, solar plexus, ribs, groin, thighs, knees, shins, and instep.

Arm Lock - A joint lock applied to the arm.

Assailant - A person who threatens or attacks another.

Assault - The willful attempt or threat to inflict injury upon

284

the person of another.

Assault and Battery - The unlawful touching of another person without justification.

Assert - One of the five possible tactical responses to a threatening situation. To stand up for your rights (see Comply, Escape, De-Escalate, and Fight Back).

Assessment - The process of rapidly gathering, analyzing, and accurately evaluating information in terms of threat and danger. You can assess people, places, actions, and objects.

Attachment - The touching of the arms or legs prior to executing a trapping technique.

Attack - Offensive action designed to physically control, injure, or kill another person.

Attack By Draw - One of the five conventional methods of attack. A method of attack whereby the fighter offers his assailant an intentional opening designed to lure an attack.

Attributes of Combat - The physical, mental, and spiritual qualities that enhance combat skills and tactics.

Attribute Uniformity - Various combative attributes (i.e., speed, power, accuracy, balance, etc.) which are executed the same way every time.

Autoloader - A handgun that operates by mechanical spring pressure and recoil force that ejects the spent cartridge case and automatically feeds a fresh round from the magazine. (Also known as a Semiautomatic).

Awareness - Perception or knowledge of people, places, actions, and objects. (In CFA there are three categories of tactical awareness: Criminal Awareness, Situational Awareness, and Self-Awareness.)

Axiom - A truth that is self-evident.

B

Back Position - One of the ground fighting positions. The back position is assumed when your chest is on top of your assailant's back.

Back fist - A punch made with the back of the knuckles.

Back strap - The rear, vertical portion of the pistol frame.

Balance - One's ability to maintain equilibrium while stationary or moving.

Barrier - Any large object that can be used to obstruct an attacker's path or angle of attack.

Blading the Body - Strategically positioning your body at a 45-degree angle.

Block - A defensive tool designed to intercept the assailant's attack by placing a non-vital target between the assailant's strike and your vital body target.

Bludgeon - Any club like weapon used for offensive and defensive purposes (e.g., baseball bat, club, pipe, crowbar, heavy tree branch, etc.) Bludgeons are usually heavier and thicker than sticks.

Body Composition - The ratio of fat to lean body tissue.

Body Language - Nonverbal communication through posture, gestures, and facial expressions.

Body Mechanics - Technically precise body movement during the execution of a body weapon, defensive technique, or other fighting maneuver.

Body Weapon - One of the various body parts that can be used to strike or otherwise injure or kill a criminal assailant. (Also known as Tool).

Bore - The inside of the barrel of a firearm.

Boxing - (See Western Boxing).

Break fall - A method of safely falling to the ground.

Burn Out - A negative emotional state acquired by physically over training. Some symptoms of burn-out include: physical illness, boredom, anxiety, disinterest in training, and general sluggish behavior.

Bushido - The ancient and honorable code of the samurai or warrior.

C

Cadence - Coordinating tempo and rhythm to establish a timing pattern of movement.

Caliber - The diameter of a projectile.

Cardiorespiratory Conditioning - A component of physical fitness that deals with the heart, lungs, and circulatory system.

Carriage - The way you carry yourself.

Cartridge - A cylindrical case containing components of a round of ammunition: case, primer, powder charge, and bullet.

Center-Fire - A type of firearm cartridge that has its primer located in the center of the case bottom.

Centerline - An imaginary vertical line that divides your body in half and which contains many of your vital anatomical targets.

Center Mass - The center portion of the torso.

Chamber - 1) The part of a firearm in which a cartridge is contained at the instant of firing. 2) The raising of the knee to execute a kick.

Choice Words - (See Selective Semantics.)

Choke - A close quarter (grappling range) technique that requires one to apply pressure to either the trachea of carotid arteries.

Circular Movement - Movements that follow the direction of a curve.

Close Quarter Combat - One of the three ranges of knife and bludgeon combat. At this distance, you can strike, slash, or stab your assailant with a variety of close-quarter techniques.

Close to Contact Shooting - Discharging a firearm with the muzzle approximately one inch distance from the target.

Cognitive Development - One of the five elements of CFA's mental component. The process of developing and enhancing your fighting skills through specific mental exercises and techniques. (see Analysis and Integration, Killer Instinct, Philosophy and Strategic/Tactical Development.)

Cognitive Domain - This encompasses the specific concepts, principles and knowledge required to use your combative tools or techniques effectively.

Cognitive Exercises - Various mental exercises used to enhance fighting skills and tactics.

Combat Arts - The various arts of war. (See Martial Arts.) Combative Attributes - (See Attributes.)

Combative Fitness - A state characterized by cardiorespiratory and muscular/ skeletal conditioning, as well as proper body composition.

Combative Mentality - A combative state of mind necessary for fighting. Also known as the Killer Instinct. (see Killer Instinct.)

Combat Ranges - The various ranges of armed and unarmed combat.

Combative Power - The ability of capacity to perform or act effectively in combat.

Combative Truth - A combative element that conforms to fact or actuality and which is proven to be true.

Combative Utility - The quality of condition of being combatively useful. Combination(s) - (See Compound Attack.)

Come-Along - A series of holds or joint locks that force your adversary to move in any direction you desire.

Coming to a Base - The process of getting up to your hands and knees from the prone position.

Common Peroneal Nerve - A pressure point area located approximately four to six inches above the knee on the midline of the outside of the thigh.

Completion Phase - One of the three stages of a stick or bludgeon strike. The completion phase is the completion point of a swing.

Comply - One of the five tactical responses to a threatening situation. To obey an assailant's demands. (see Assert, De-Escalate, Escape, and Fight Back.)

Composure - A combative attribute. Composure is a quiet and focused mind set that enables you to acquire your combative agenda.

Compound Attack - One of the five conventional methods of attack. Two or more body weapons launched in strategic succession whereby the fighter overwhelms his assailant with a flurry of full speed, full force blows. (see Indirect Attack, Immobilization Attack, Attack By Draw, and Single Attack.)

Concealment - Not being visible to your adversary.

Conditioning Training - A CFA training methodology requiring the practitioner to deliver a variety of offensive and defensive combinations for a four minute period (see Proficiency Training and Street Training.)

Confrontation Evasion - Strategically manipulating the distance or environment to avoid a possible confrontation.

Congruency - The state of harmoniously orchestrating the verbal and non verbal de-escalation principles.

Contact Evasion - Physically moving or manipulating your body targets to avoid being struck (i.e., slipping your head to the side or side stepping from a charging assailant).

Contact Shooting - Discharging a firearm with the muzzle touching the target.

Contemporary Fighting Arts® (CFA) - A modern martial art and self-defense system made up of three parts: physical, mental, and spiritual.

Conventional Ground Fighting Tools - Specific ground fighting techniques designed to control, restrain and temporarily incapacitate your adversary. Some conventional ground fighting tactics include: submission holds, locks, certain choking techniques, and specific striking techniques.

Cool-down - A series of light exercises and movements that immediately follow a workout. The purpose of the cool-down is to hasten the removal of metabolic wastes and gradually return the heart to its resting rate.

Coordination - A physical attribute characterized by the ability to perform a technique or movement with efficiency, balance, and accuracy.

Counterattack - Offensive action made to counter an assailant's initial attack.

Courage - A combative attribute. The state of mind and spirit that enables a fighter to face danger and vicissitudes with confidence, resolution, and bravery.

Courageousness - (See Courage).

Cover - Any object that protects you from gunfire.

Criminal Awareness - One of the three categories of CFA awareness. It involves a general understanding and knowledge of the nature and dynamics of a criminal's motivations, mentalities, methods, and capabilities to perpetrate violent crime. (see Situational Awareness and Self-Awareness.)

Criminal Justice - The study of criminal law and the procedures associated with its enforcement.

Criminology - The scientific study of crime and criminals.

Criss Cross - An entry maneuver which allows you to

travel across a threshold quickly while employing a correct ready weapon position.

Cross Stepping - The process of crossing one foot in front or behind the other when moving.

Crushing Tactics - Nuclear grappling range techniques designed to crush the assailant's anatomical targets.

Cutting Accuracy - The ability to cut your assailant with precision and exactness.

Cutting Makeshift Weapon - One of the four types of CFA makeshift weapons. Any object or implement that can be used to effectively stab or slash an assailant. (see also Distracting Makeshift Weapon, Shielding Makeshift Weapon, and Striking Makeshift Weapon.)

Cylinder - The part of a revolver that holds cartridges in individual chambers.

D

Deadly Force - Weapons or techniques that may result in imminent, unconsciousness, permanent disfigurement, or death.

Deadly Weapon - An instrument designed to inflict serious bodily injury or death (e.g., firearms, impact tools, edged weapons).

Deception - A combative attribute. A stratagem whereby you delude your assailant.

Decisiveness - A combative attribute. The ability to follow a tactical course of action that is unwavering and focused.

De-escalation - One of the five possible tactical responses to a threatening situation. The science and art of diffusing a hostile individual without resorting to physical force. (see Assert, Comply, Escape and Fight Back).

De-escalation Stance - One of the many strategic stances used in the CFA system. A strategic and non aggressive stance used when diffusing a hostile individual.

Defense - The ability to strategically thwart an assailant's attack (armed or unarmed).

Defensive Flow - A progression of continuous defensive responses. Defensive Mentality - A defensive mind-set.

Defensive Range Manipulation (DRM) - The strategic manipulation of ranges (armed or unarmed) for defensive purposes.

Defensive Reaction Time - The elapsed time between an assailant's physical attack and your defensive response to that attack (see Offensive Reaction Time).

Demeanor - One of the essential factors to consider when assessing a threatening individual. A person's outward behavior.

Dependency - The dangerous phenomenon of solely relying on a particular person, agency, instrument, device, tool, animal, or weapon for self-defense and personal protection.

Destructions - A technique that strikes the assailant's attacking limb. Diet - A life-style of healthy eating.

Distance Gap - The spatial gap between the different ranges of armed and unarmed combat.

Distancing - The ability to quickly understand spatial relationships and how they relate to combat.

Distracting Makeshift Weapon - One of the four types of CFA makeshift weapons. An object that can be thrown into an assailant's face, body, or legs to distract him temporarily (see Cutting Makeshift Weapon, Striking Makeshift Weapon, and Shielding Makeshift Weapon.)

Distraction Tactics - Various verbal and physical tactics designed to distract your adversary.

Dojo - The Japanese term for "training hall."

Dominant Eye - The eye which is primarily used for aiming a firearm. The dominant eye is the one which is stronger and does more work.

Double-Action - A type of pistol action in which squeezing the trigger will both cock and release the hammer.

Drake Shooting - Shooting into places of likely cover.

Dry Firing - The process of shooting an unloaded firearm.

Duck - A defensive technique that permits you to evade your assailant's strike. Ducking is performed by dropping your body down and forward to avoid the assailant's blow.

E

Ectomorph - A body type classified by a high degree of slenderness, angularity, and fragility (see Endomorph and Mesomorph).

Effectiveness - One of the three criteria for a CFA body weapon, technique, tactic or maneuver. It means the ability to produce a desired effect (see Efficiency and Safety).

Efficiency - One of the three criteria for a CFA body weapon, technique, tactic or maneuver. It means the ability to reach an objective quickly and economically (see Effectiveness and Safety).

Ejector - The part of a pistol which ejects empty cartridge cases.

Embracing the Range - A ground fighting tactic whereby you pull or embrace your assailant.

Emotional Control - One of the nonverbal principles of strategic de-escalation. The ability to remain calm when faced with a hostile or threatening person.

Emotionless - A combative attribute. Being temporarily devoid of human feeling.

Endomorph - A body type classified by a high degree of roundness, softness, and body fat (see Ectomorph and Mesomorph).

Entry Method - A method that permits you to safely enter a combat range. Entry Technique - A technique that permits you to safely enter a combat range.

Entry Tool - A tool that permits you to safely enter a combat range.

Escape - Also known as tactical retreat. One of the five possible tactical responses to a threatening situation. To flee rapidly from the threat or danger. (See Comply, De-Escalate, Assert and Fight Back).

Escape Routes - Various avenues or exits that permit you to escape from a threatening individual or situation.

Evasion - A defensive maneuver that allows you to strategically maneuver your body away from the assailant's strike.

Evasive Sidestepping - Evasive footwork where the practitioner moves to either the right or left side.

Evasiveness - A combative attribute. The ability of avoid threat or danger. Evolution - A gradual process of change.

Excessive Force - An amount of force that exceeds the need for a particular event and is unjustified in the eyes of the law.

Experimentation - The painstaking process of testing a combative hypothesis or theory.

Explosiveness - A combative attribute that is characterized by a sudden outburst of violent energy.

F

Fake - Body movements that disguise your attack. This includes movements of the eyes, head, shoulders, knees, feet and in some cases the voice.

Fatal Funnel - A danger area that is created by openings such as doorways, windows, hallways, stairwells, etc.

Feed - (See Attachment.)

Fear - A strong and unpleasant emotion caused by the anticipation or awareness of threat or danger. There are three stages of fear in order of intensity: Fright, Panic, and Terror. (see Fright, Panic, Terror).

Feeler - A tool that tests the assailant's reaction time and overall abilities.

Feint - A tool that draws an offensive reaction from the assailant, thereby opening him up for a real strike. Feints are different from fakes because they are performed through the movement of an actual limb.

Femoral Nerve - A pressure point area located approximately six inches above the knee on the inside of the thigh.

Fight Back - One of the five possible tactical responses to a threatening situation. To use various physical and psychological tactics to either incapacitate or terminate a criminal assailant. (See Comply, Escape, Assert and De-Escalate.)

Fighting Stance - One of the different types of stances used in CFA's system. A strategic posture you can assume when face-to-face with an unarmed assailant (s). (See De-escalation Stance, Knife Defense Stance, Knife Fighting Stance, Firearms Stance, Natural Stance, Stick Fighting Stance).

Fight-or-Flight Syndrome - A response of the sympathetic nervous system to a fearful and threatening situation, during which it prepares your body to either fight or flee from the perceived danger.

Finesse - A combative attribute. The ability to skillfully execute a movement or a series of movements with grace and refinement.

Firearm Follow Through - Continuing to employ the shooting fundamentals throughout the delivery of your shot.

First Strike Principle (FSP) - A CFA principle which states that when physical danger is imminent and you have no other tactical option but to fight back, you should strike first, strike fast, and strike with authority.

Flexibility - The muscles' ability to move through maximum natural ranges (see Muscular/Skeletal Conditioning).

Follow - A defensive technique used in the mid to long range of knife combat.

Forms - Traditional martial arts training methodology whereby the practitioner performs a series of prearranged movements that are based upon a response to imaginary opponents (see Kata).

Formlessness - A principle that rejects the essence of structure or system.

Footwork - Quick, economical steps performed on the balls of the feet while you are relaxed, alert, and balanced. Footwork is structured around four general movements: forward, backward, right, and left.

Fractal Cognizance -Being knowledgeable and aware of the fractal ranges and tools of combat.

Fright - The first stage of fear; quick and sudden fear (see Panic and Terror).

G

Gi - A traditional martial art uniform constructed of heavy cotton canvas material. The gi is commonly worn by practitioners of karate, judo, aikido, and jujitsu.

Grappling Range - One of the three ranges of unarmed combat. Grappling range is the closest distance of unarmed combat from which you can employ a wide variety of close-quarter tools and techniques. The grappling range of unarmed combat is also divided into two different planes: vertical (standing) and horizontal (ground fighting). (see Kicking Range and Punching Range)

Grappling Range Tools - The various body tools and techniques that are employed in the grappling range of unarmed combat, including head butts; biting, tearing, clawing, crushing, and gouging tactics; foot stomps, horizontal, vertical, and diagonal elbow strikes, vertical and diagonal knee strikes, chokes, strangles, joint locks, and holds. (see and Kicking Range Tools).

Grapevine - A stabilizing technique used during a ground fight. The grapevine can be applied when you have either one (single leg grapevine) or both (double leg grapevine) of your feet hooked around the assailant's legs.

Ground Fighting - Fighting that takes place on the ground. (Also known as horizontal grappling plane).

Guard - 1) A fighter's hand positioning. 2) One of the positions used in ground fighting. The guard is a scissors hold applied with the legs.

H

Hammer - The moving part of a gun causes the firing pin to strike the cartridge primer.

Hammer Grip - A hand grip used to hold an edged weapon, bludgeon and some makeshift weapons; assumed when the top of the bludgeon or the tip of the edged weapon is pointing upwards.

Handgun - A firearm that can be held and discharged with one hand. Hand Positioning - (See Guard.)

Hang fire - A perceptible delay in the ignition of a cartridge after the primer has been struck.

Head-Hunter - A fighter who primarily attacks the head.

High-Line Kick - One of the two different classifications of a kick. A kick that is directed to targets above an assailant's waist level. (See Low-Line Kick.)

Histrionics - The field of theatrics or acting.

Homicide - The death of another person without legal justification of excuse.

Hook Kick - A circular kick that can be delivered in both kicking and punching ranges.

Hook Punch - A circular punch that can be delivered in both the punching and grappling ranges.

Hold - A specific manner of grasping or holding an assailant.

Human Shield - Using your assailant's body as a shield or obstacle in combat.

I

Ice Pick Grip - A hand grip used to hold an edged weapon, bludgeon and some makeshift weapons; assumed when the tip of the edged weapon or the top of the bludgeon is pointing downward.

Ice Pick Stick Strangle - A stick strangle used with an ice pick grip.

Immobilization Attack - One of the five conventional methods of attack. A highly complex system of moves and countermoves that allows you to temporarily control and manipulate the assailant's limbs (usually his arms and hands) in order to create an opening of attack.

Impact Power - Destructive force generated by mass and velocity.

Impact Training - A training exercise that develops pain tolerance.

Incapacitate - To disable an assailant by rendering him unconscious or damaging his bones, joints or organs.

Indirect Attack - One of the five conventional methods of attack. A progressive method of attack whereby the initial tool or technique is designed to set the assailant up for follow-up blows.

Initiation Phase - One of the three stages of a stick or bludgeon strike. The initiation phase is initiation point of a swing.

Insertion Points - Specific anatomical targets you can stab with a knife and some makeshift weapons.

Inside Position - The area between both of your assailant's arms where he has the greatest amount of control.

Intent - One of the essential factors to consider when assessing a threatening individual. The assailant's purpose or motive (see Demeanor, Positioning, Range, and Weapon Capability).

Intuition - The innate ability to know or sense something without the use of rational thought.

Intuitive Tool Response (ITR) - Spontaneously reacting with the appropriate combative tool.

J

Jab - A quick, probing punch designed to create openings in the assailant's defense.

Jeet Kune Do - "Way of Intercepting Fist." Bruce Lee's approach to the martial arts, which includes his innovative concepts, theories, methodologies, and philosophies of unarmed combat.

Joint Lock - A grappling range technique that immobilizes the assailant's joint.

Judo - "Gentle Way." A Japanese grappling art (founded by Jigoro Kano in 1882) which is used as a sport. Judo utilizes shoulder and hip throws, foot sweeps, chokes, and pins.

Jujitsu - "Gentleness" or "suppleness." A system of self-defense that is the parent of both Judo and Aikido. Jujitsu specializes in grappling range but is known to employ a few striking techniques.

K

Karate - "Empty hand" or "China hand," a traditional martial art that originated in Okinawa and later spread to Japan and Korea (see Kung-Fu).

Kata - "Pattern" or "Form". A traditional training methodology whereby the practitioner practices a series of prearranged movements.

Kick - 1) A sudden, forceful strike with the foot (see High-Line Kick and Low- Line Kick); 2) The recoil of a firearm.

Kick boxing - A popular combat sport that employs full-contact tools.

Kicking Range - One of the three ranges of unarmed combat. Kicking range is the furthest distance of unarmed combat wherein you use your legs to strike an assailant. (see Grappling Range and Punching Range).

Kicking Range Tools - The various body weapons employed in the kicking range of unarmed combat, including side kicks, push kicks, hook kicks, and vertical kicks.

Killer Instinct - A cold, primal mentality that surges to your consciousness and turns you into a vicious fighter.

Kinesics - The study of nonlinguistic body movement communications (i.e., eye movement, shrugs, facial gestures, etc.).

Kinesiology - The study of principles and mechanics of human movement.

Kinesthetic Perception - The ability to accurately feel your body during the execution of a particular movement.

Kneeling Firearm Stance - A strategic stance you assume when kneeling down with a handgun.

Knife-Defense Stance - One of the many stances used in CFA's system. A strategic stance you assume when face-to-face with an knife or edged weapon attacker. (See De-escalation Stance, Fighting Stance, Knife Fighting Stance, Firearms Stance, Natural Stance, Stick Fighting Stance).

Kung-Fu - "Accomplished task or effort," a term used erroneously to identify the traditional Chinese martial arts (see Karate).

L

Lead Side -The side of the body that faces an assailant.

Leg Block - A blocking technique used with the legs. The leg block can be angled in three different directions: forward, right and left.

Limited Penetration - The (LP) is a corner clearing movement performed by positioning your firearm and one eye around the corner.

Linear Movement - Movements that follow the path of a straight line.

Long Range Combat - The furthest distance of knife and bludgeon combat. At this distance you can only strike or slash your assailant's hand.

Low Maintenance Tool - Offensive and defensive tools that require the least amount of training and practice to maintain proficiency. Low maintenance tools generally don't require preliminary stretching.

Low-Line Kick - One of the two different classifications of a kick. A kick that is directed to targets below the assailant's waist level. (See High-Line Kick.)

Lock - (see Joint Lock).

Loyalty - The state of being faithful to a person, cause, or ideal.

M

Makeshift Weapon - A common everyday object that can be converted into either an offensive or defensive weapon. There are four Makeshift Weapon classifications in the CFA system: Cutting Makeshift Weapons, Shielding Makeshift Weapons, Distracting Makeshift Weapons, and Striking Makeshift Weapons.

Maneuver - To manipulate into a strategically desired position.

Manipulation Accuracy - The ability to manipulate your assailant's limbs and joints with precision and exactness.

Martial Artist - One who studies and practices the martial arts.

Martial Arts - The traditional "arts of war" (see Karate and Kung-Fu).

Martial Truth - (See Combative Truth.)

Mechanics - (See Body Mechanics.)

Medicine Ball - A large, heavy ball used to strengthen and condition a fighter's stomach muscles.

Meet - A defensive technique that intercepts your assailant's line of attack with a slash.

Mental Attributes - The various cognitive qualities that enhance your fighting skills.

Mental Component - One of the three vital components of the CFA system. The mental component includes the cerebral aspects of fighting including the Killer Instinct, Strategic & Tactical Development, Analysis & Integration, Philosophy and Cognitive Development (see Physical Component and Spiritual Component).

Mesomorph - A body type classified by a high degree of muscularity and strength. (see Endomorph and Ectomorph).

Methods of Attack - The five conventionally recognized

methods of attacking. They include: single attack, indirect attack, attack by draw, immobilization attack, and compound attack.

Mexican Standoff - A precarious situation where both you and your adversary have the drop on one another.

Mid Phase - One of the three stages of a stick swing. The mid phase is the contact or impact point of the swing.

Mid Range Combat - One of the three ranges of knife and bludgeon combat. At this distance you can strike, slash or stab your assailant's head, arms and body with your weapon.

Misfire - A failure of a cartridge to fire after the primer has been struck.

Mobility - A combative attribute. The ability to move your body quickly and freely while balanced. (see Footwork).

Modern Martial Art - A pragmatic combat art that has evolved to meet the demands and characteristics of the present time.

Modernist - One who subscribes to the philosophy of the modern martial arts.

Modification - To make fundamental changes to serve a new end.

Mounted Position - One of the five general ground fighting positions. The mounted position is where the practitioner sits on top of his assailant's torso or chest.

Mouthpiece - A rubber protector used to cover your teeth when sparring. There are two types of mouthpiece: single and double.

Muscular Endurance - The muscles' ability to perform the same motion or task repeatedly for a prolonged period of time.

Muscular Flexibility - The muscles' ability to move through maximum natural ranges.

Muscular Strength - The maximum force that can be

exerted by a particular muscle or muscle group against resistance.

Muscular/Skeletal Conditioning - An element of physical fitness that entails muscular strength, endurance, and flexibility.

Muzzle - The front end of the barrel.

Muzzle Flash - An incandescent burst of light which is emitted from the muzzle and cylinder of a handgun.

N

Natural Stance - One of the many stances used in CFA's system. A strategic stance you assume when approached by a suspicious person who appears non threatening. (See De-escalation Stance, Fighting Stance, Knife Fighting Stance, Firearms Stance, Knife-Defense Stance, and Stick Fighting Stance).

Neutralize - (See Incapacitate.)

Neutral Zone - The distance outside of the kicking range from which neither the practitioner nor the assailant can touch the other.

Nomenclature Awareness - The ability to understand and recognize the system of names used in combat.

Non aggressive Physiology - Strategic body language used to de-escalate a potentially violent individual.

Non telegraphic Movement - Body mechanics or movements that do not inform an assailant of your intentions.

Nuclear Ground Fighting Tools - Specific grappling range tools designed to inflict immediate and irreversible damage. Some nuclear tools and tactics include: (1) Biting tactics; (2) Tearing tactics; (3) Crushing tactics; (4) Continuous Choking tactics; (5) Gouging techniques; (6) Raking tactics; (7) And all striking techniques.

O

OC (Oleoresin Capsicum, also known as pepper gas) - A natural mixture of oil and cayenne pepper used as a self-defense spray. OC is an inflammatory agent that affects the assailant's mucus membranes (i.e. eyes, nose, throat, lungs).

Offense - The armed and unarmed means and methods of attacking a criminal assailant.

Offensive Flow - A progression of continuous offensive movements or actions designed to neutralize or terminate your adversary. (see Compound Attack).

Offensive Range Manipulation (ORM) - The strategic manipulation of ranges (armed or unarmed) for offensive purposes.

Offensive Reaction Time (ORT) - The elapsed time between target selection and target impaction.

One-Hand Reloading - The process of reloading a firearm with only one hand.

One-Mindedness - A state of deep concentration wherein you are free from all distractions (internal and external).

Opposite Poles - One of the ground fighting positions. The opposite pole position is assumed when both you and your assailant are facing opposite directions. This often occurs when sprawling against your adversary.

Ornamental Techniques - Techniques that are characterized as complex, inefficient, and or impractical for real combat situations.

P

Pain Tolerance - Your ability to physically and psychologically withstand pain. 490

Palming - The strategic concealment of a knife or edged weapon behind the forearm. Also known as Knife Palming.

Panic - The second stage of fear; overpowering fear (see

Fright and Terror).

Parry - A defensive technique; a quick, forceful slap that redirects an assailant's linear attack.

Pass - A defensive technique used in knife fighting.

Patience - A combative attribute. The ability to endure and tolerate difficulty.

Perception - Interpretation of vital information acquired from your senses when faced with a potentially threatening situation.

Perpendicular Mount - One of the five general ground fighting positions. The perpendicular mount is established when you are lying on top of your adversary and both of your legs are on one side of his body.

Philosophical Resolution - The act of analyzing and answering various questions concerning the use of violence in defense of yourself and others.

Philosophy - One of the five aspects of CFA's mental component. A deep state of introspection whereby you methodically resolve critical questions concerning the use of force in defense of yourself or others.

Physical Attributes - The numerous physical qualities that enhance your combative skills and abilities.

Physical Component - One of the three vital components of the CFA system. The physical component includes the physical aspects of fighting including Physical Fitness, Weapon/Technique Mastery, and Combative Attributes (see Mental Component and Spiritual Component).

Physical Conditioning - (See Combative Fitness).

Pistol - A gun with a short barrel that can be held, aimed, and fired with one hand.

Power - A physical attribute of armed and unarmed combat. The amount of force you can generate when striking an anatomical target.

Physical Fitness - (See Combative Fitness).

Pitch - One of the four components of the human voice. The relative highness or lowness of the voice.

Poker Face - A neutral and attentive facial expression that is used when de- escalating a hostile individual. The poker face prevents a hostile person from reading your intentions or feelings.

Positioning - The spatial relationship of the assailant to the assailed person in terms of target exposure, escape, angle of attack, and various other strategic considerations.

Positions of Concealment - Various objects or locations that permit you to temporarily hide from your adversary. Positions of Concealment are most commonly used to evade engagement with your assailant(s) and they permit you to attack with the element of surprise. Positions of Concealment include: trees, shrubbery, behind doors, the dark, walls, stairwells, under cars, large and tall objects, etc.

Positions of Cover - Any object or location that temporarily protects you from the assailant's gun fire. Some Positions of Cover include: large concrete utility poles, large rocks, thick trees, an engine block, corner of a building, concrete steps, etc.

Post Traumatic Syndrome (PTS) - A group of symptoms that may occur in the aftermath of a violent confrontation with a criminal assailant. Common symptoms of Post Traumatic Syndrome include denial, shock, fear, anger, severe depression, sleeping and eating disorders, societal withdrawal, and paranoia.

Power Generator - (See Anatomical Power Generators)

Premise - An axiom, concept, rule or any other valid reason to modify or go beyond that which has been established.

Pressure Point - A point on the body where a nerve lies

close to its surface and it is supported by bone or muscle mass.

Probable Reaction Dynamics (PRD) - the opponent's anticipated or predicted movements or actions during both armed and unarmed combat.

Probe -A offensive tool that tests the assailant's combative abilities.

Proficiency Training - A CFA training methodology requiring the practitioner to execute a specific body weapon, technique, maneuver or tactic over and over for a prescribed number or repetitions (see Conditioning Training and Street Training).

Progressive Indirect Attack -(see Indirect Attack).

Proxemics - The study of the nature and effect of man's personal space.

Proximity - The ability to maintain a strategically safe distance from a threatening individual.

Pseudospeciation - A combative attribute. The tendency to assign subhuman and inferior qualities to a threatening assailant.

Psychological Conditioning - The process of conditioning the mind for the horrors and rigors of real combat.

Psycho/Emotional Training - Combative training conducted when you're experiencing different types of emotional states.

Psychomotor Domain - This includes the physical skills and attributes necessary to execute a combative tool, technique or maneuver.

Psychopath - A person with an antisocial personality disorder, especially one manifested in aggressive, perverted, criminal, or amoral behavior.

Pummel - A flurry of full-speed, full-force strikes delivered from the mounted position.

Punch - A quick, forceful strike of the fists.

Punching Range - One of the three ranges of unarmed combat. Punching range is the mid range of unarmed combat from which the fighter uses his hands to strike his assailant. (see Kicking Range and Grappling Range)

Punching Range Tools - The various body weapons that are employed in the punching range of unarmed combat, including finger jabs, palm heel strikes, rear cross, knife hand strikes, horizontal and shovel hooks, uppercuts, and hammer fist strikes. (see Grappling Range Tools and Kicking Range Tools).

Q

Qualities of Combat - (see Attributes of Combat).

Quick Peek - A technique which is executed from a position of cover by rapidly darting out a small portion of your head and one eye to quickly observe.

R

Range - The spatial relationship between a fighter and a threatening assailant.

Range Deficiency - The inability to effectively fight and defend in all ranges (armed and unarmed) of combat.

Range Manipulation - A combative attribute. The strategic manipulation of combat ranges.

Range Proficiency - A combative attribute. The ability to effectively fight and defend in all ranges (armed and unarmed) of combat.

Ranges of Armed Combat - The various distances a fighter might physically engage with an assailant while involved in armed combat: including knives, bludgeons, projectiles, make-shift weapons, and firearms.)

Ranges of Engagement - (See Combat Ranges).

Ranges of Unarmed Combat - The three distances a fighter might physically engage with an assailant while involved in unarmed combat: kicking range, punching range, and grappling range.

Reaction Dynamics - The assailant's physical response to a particular tool, technique, or weapon after initial contact is made.

Reaction Time - The elapsed time between a stimulus and the response to that particular stimulus (see Offensive Reaction Time and Defensive Reaction Time).

Rear Cross - A straight punch delivered from the rear hand that crosses from right to left (if in a left stance) or left to right (if in a right stance).

Rear Side - The side of the body furthest from the assailant (see Lead Side).

Reasonable Force - That degree of force which is not excessive for a particular event and which is appropriate in protecting yourself or others.

Refinement - The strategic and methodical process of improving or perfecting.

Repetition - Performing a single movement, exercise, strike or action continuously for a specific period.

Research - A scientific investigation or inquiry.

Rest Position - A relaxed posture you assume (when holding a stick or bludgeon) during idle periods in class (i.e., talking to another students, receiving instructions, etc.).

Reverberation Path - The path at which your stick or bludgeon can bounce back at you.

Revolver - A handgun consisting of a cylinder that brings several chambers successively into line with the barrel of the gun.

Rhythm - Movements characterized by the natural ebb and flow of related elements.

Right to Bear Arms - A provision of the Second Amendment to the United States Constitution that prohibits our government from interfering with the right of the people to arm themselves.

Rimfire - A firearm cartridge which has its primer located around the rim of the case bottom.

Round - 1) A period of time. 2) A single unit of ammunition (see Cartridge).

S

Safe Room - A strategic location in your residence where you and family members can escape from an intruder who has entered your home.

Safety - One of the three criteria for a CFA body weapon, technique, maneuver or tactic. It means the that the tool, technique, maneuver or tactic provides the least amount of danger and risk for the practitioner (see Efficiency and Effectiveness).

Scissors Hold - (see Guard).

Secondary Hand - A close quarter technique used in both knife and bludgeon fighting whereby you temporarily hold your assailant's weapon hand in place after you have employed a defensive maneuver.

Secondary Weapons - Various natural body weapons that are applied during armed combat.

Selective Semantics - The selection and utilization of strategic words to de-escalate a hostile person. Also known as Choice Words.

Self-Awareness - One of the three categories of CFA awareness. Knowing and understanding yourself. This includes aspects of yourself which may provoke criminal violence and which will promote a proper and strong reaction to an attack. (see Criminal Awareness and Situational Awareness.)

Self-Confidence - Having trust and faith in yourself.

Self-Defense - The act of defending yourself or one's family (also called Personal Protection or Self-Protection).

Self-Enlightenment - The state of knowing your capabilities, limitations, character traits, feelings, general attributes, and motivations (see Self- Awareness.)

Semiautomatic Handgun - (see Autoloader).

Sensei - Teacher.

Set - A term used to describe a grouping of repetitions.

Setup Tool - A tool used to throw the assailant off balance and/or open his defenses.

Shadow Fighting - A CFA training exercise used to develop and refine your tools, techniques, and attributes of armed and unarmed combat.

Shielding Makeshift Weapon - One of the four types of CFA makeshift weapons. Any object that can be used to effectively shield oneself from an assailant's attack (see also Distracting Makeshift Weapon, Cutting Makeshift Weapon, and Striking Makeshift Weapon.)

Shooting Accuracy - The ability to shoot a firearm with precision and exactness.

Shot - A package or wad of metal balls that vary in size and spread out as they travel away from the muzzle of a shot gun.

Shotgun - A single-or double-barreled, smooth-bore firearm used for firing shot or slugs at a relatively close distance.

Shoulder Roll - A defensive technique that rocks your body away from a punch in order to nullify its force.

Side Fall - A firearm engagement technique which is executed from a kneeling position behind cover.

Sifu - (See Sensei.)

Sight Alignment - A component of marksmanship whereby you correctly align your dominant eye with both the front and rear sights of your firearm.

Sights - Various electronic, optical, and mechanical devices used to aim a firearm.

Single Action - A type of pistol action in which pulling the trigger will release the hammer.

Single Attack - One of the five conventional methods of attack. A method of attack whereby you deliver a solitary offensive strike. It may involve a series of discreet probes or one swift, powerful strike aimed at terminating the encounter. (See Compound Attack, Indirect Attack, Immobilization Attack, and Attack By Draw).

Situational Awareness - One of the three categories of CFA awareness. A state of being totally alert to your immediate surroundings, including people, places, objects, and actions. (see Criminal Awareness and Self-Awareness.)

Skeletal Alignment - The proper alignment or arrangement of your body. Skeletal Alignment maximizes the structural integrity of striking tools.

Slash - One of the two ways to cut someone with a knife or edged weapon. A quick, sweeping stroke of a knife (see Stab.)

Slipping - A defensive maneuver that permits you to avoid an assailant's linear blow without stepping out of range. Slipping can be accomplished by quickly snapping the head and upper torso sideways (right or left) to avoid the blow.

Snap Back - A defensive maneuver that permits you to avoid an assailant's linear and circular blow without stepping out of range. The snap back can be accomplished by quickly snapping the head backwards to avoid the assailant's blow.

Somatotyping - A method of classifying human body types or builds into three different categories: ectomorph, mesomorph, and endomorph.

Speed - A physical attribute of armed and unarmed combat. The rate or a measure of the rapid rate of motion.

Spinning Kicks - Kicks delivered with a spin of the body.

Spinning Punches - Punches delivered with a spin of the body.

Spiritual Component - One of the three vital components of the CFA system. The spiritual component includes the metaphysical issues and aspects of existence (see Physical Component and Mental Component).

Sprawling - A defensive technique in grappling range. The sprawl technique is accomplished by lowering your hips to the ground while simultaneously shooting both of your legs back.

Square-Off - To be face-to-face with a hostile or threatening assailant who is about to attack you.

Squib Load - A cartridge which develops less than normal velocity after the ignition of a cartridge.

Stab - One of the two ways to cut someone with a knife or edged weapon. A quick thrust made with a pointed weapon or implement, usually a knife. (see Slash.)

Stable Terrain - Terrain which is principally characterized as stationary, compact, dense, hard, flat, dry, or solid.

Stance - One of the many strategic postures that you assume prior to or during armed or unarmed combat.

Stance Selection - A combative attribute. The ability to instinctively select a stance appropriate for a particular combat situation.

Standing Firearm Stance - A strategic stance you assume when standing with a handgun.

Step and Drag - Strategic footwork used when standing on

314

unstable terrain. Stick Block - A defensive technique that stops your assailant's stick strike.

Stick Deflection - A defensive technique that deflects and redirects your assailant's stick strike.

Stick Twirl - A dexterity exercise performed with either one or two sticks. Stop-Hit - A method of hitting the assailant before his tool reaches full extension.

Stopping Power - A firearm's ability to stop the assailant from continuing any further action.

Strategic Leaning - A defensive maneuver which permits you to evade a knife slash while remaining in range to counter.

Strategic Positioning - Tactically positioning yourself to either escape, move behind a barrier, or use a makeshift weapon.

Strategy - A carefully planned method of achieving your goal of engaging an assailant under advantageous conditions.

Street Fight - A spontaneous and violent confrontation between two or more individuals wherein no rules apply.

Street Fighter - An unorthodox combatant who has no formal training. His combative skills and tactics are usually developed in the street by the process of trial and error.

Street Smarts - Having the knowledge, skills and attitude necessary to avoid, defuse, confront, and neutralize both armed and unarmed assailants.

Street Training - A CFA training methodology requiring the practitioner to deliver explosive compound attacks for ten to twenty seconds (see Conditioning Training and Proficiency Training).

Strength Training - The process of developing muscular strength through systematic application of progressive resistance.

Striking Accuracy - The ability to strike your assailant with precision and exactness (this includes natural body weapons, bludgeons and some makeshift weapons).

Striking Art - A combat art that relies predominantly on striking techniques to neutralize or terminate a criminal attacker.

Striking Tool - 1) A natural body weapon that impacts with the assailant's anatomical target. 2) A hand-held implement that impacts with the assailant's anatomical target.

Striking Makeshift Weapon - One of the four types of CFA makeshift weapons. Any object that can be used to effectively strike a criminal assailant (see also Distracting Makeshift Weapon, Cutting Makeshift Weapon, and Shielding Makeshift Weapon.)

Strong Side - The strongest and most coordinated side of your body. Structure - A definite and organized pattern.

Style - The distinct manner in which a fighter executes or performs his combat skills.

Stylistic Integration - The purposeful and scientific collection of tools and techniques from various disciplines, which are strategically integrated and dramatically altered to meet three essential criteria: efficiency, effectiveness, and combative safety.

System - The unification of principles, philosophies, rules, strategies, methodologies, tools, and techniques or a particular method of combat.

T

Tactical Calming - (See De-Escalation.)

Tactic - The skill of using the available means to achieve an end.

Tactical Option Selection - A combative attribute. The ability to select the appropriate tactical option for any particular self-defense situation.

Tactile Sight - A combative attribute. The ability to "see" through tactile contact with your assailant.

Takedowns -Various grappling maneuvers designed to take your assailant down to the ground.

Target Exploitation - A combative attribute. The strategic maximization of your assailant's reaction dynamics during a fight. Target Exploitation can be applied in both armed and unarmed encounters.

Target Impaction - The successful striking of the appropriate anatomical target.

Target Orientation - A combative attribute. Having a workable knowledge of the assailant's anatomical targets. Target orientation is divided into five different categories: (1) Impact Targets - anatomical targets that can be struck with your natural body weapons; (2) Non-Impact Targets - anatomical targets that can be strangled, twisted, torn, crushed, clawed, gouged, broken, dislocated, or strategically manipulated; (3) Edged Weapon Targets - anatomical targets that can be punctured or slashed with a knife or edged weapon; (4) Bludgeon Targets - anatomical targets that can be struck with a stick or bludgeon; (5) Ballistic Targets - anatomical targets that can be shot by a firearm.

Target Recognition - The ability to immediately recognize appropriate anatomical targets during an emergency self-defense situation.

Target Selection - The process of mentally selecting the appropriate anatomical target for your self-defense situation. This is predicated on certain factors, including proper force response, assailant's positioning and range.

Target Stare - A form of telegraphing whereby you stare at the anatomical target you intend to strike.

Target Zones - The three areas which an assailant's anatomical targets are located. (See Zone One, Zone Two and Zone Three.)

Technique - A systematic procedure by which a task is accomplished.

Telegraphic Cognizance - A combative attribute. The ability to recognize both verbal and non-verbal signs of aggression or assault.

Telegraphing - Unintentionally making your intentions known to your adversary. Tempo - The speed or rate at which you speak.

Terrain - The type of surface that you are standing on. There are two classifications of terrain: stable and unstable. (See Stable Terrain and Unstable Terrain)

Terrain Orientation - A combative attribute. Having a working knowledge of the various types of environmental terrains and their advantages, dangers, and strategic limitations.

Terror - The third stage of fear; defined as overpowering fear (see Fright and Panic).

Throw - Grappling techniques designed to unbalance your assailant and lift him off the floor.

Timing - A physical and mental attribute or armed and unarmed combat. Your ability to execute a movement at the optimum moment.

Tone - The overall quality or character of your voice.

Tool - (See Body Weapon.)

Traditional Style/System - (See Traditional Martial Art.)

Traditionalism - The beliefs and principles of a traditional or classical martial art.

Traditionalist - One who subscribes to the principles and practices of traditional martial arts.

Traditional Martial Arts - Any martial art that fails to evolve and meet the demands and characteristics of the present time (see Karate and Kung-Fu).

Training Drills - The various exercises and drills aimed at perfecting combat skills, attributes, and tactics.

Training Methodologies - Training procedures utilized in the CFA system.

Training Zone - The training zone (or target heart rate) is a safe and effective level of physical activity that produces cardiorespiratory fitness.

Trapping - Momentarily immobilizing or manipulating the assailant's limb or limbs in order to create an opening to attack.

Trapping Range - The distance between punching and grappling range in which trapping techniques are attempted.

Traversing Skills - Pivoting and twisting laterally. Traversing skills can be used for both armed and unarmed combat.

Trigger Squeeze - A component of marksmanship. Trigger Squeeze is achieved by squeezing the trigger of your firearm straight to the rear in a smooth and fluid manner without disturbing the sight alignment.

Trouble Shooting Skills - A combative attribute. The ability to immediately diagnose and solve problems when engaged with the adversary.

U

Unified Mind - A mind which is free and clear of distractions and focused on the combative situation.

Uniform Crime Report (UCR) - A nationwide cooperative statistical compilation of the efforts and reports of 16,000 state and local law enforcement agencies that voluntarily report data on crime.

Unstable Terrain - Terrain which is characterized as mobile, uneven, flexible, slippery, wet, or rocky. (See Stable Terrain).

Unstructured Modernist - A martial artist who adheres to the abstract principles of combative formlessness.

319

Use of Force Response - A combative attribute. Selecting the appropriate level of force for a particular emergency self-defense situation.

V

V-Grip - A strategically defensive grip used to defend against an edged weapon attack.

Vertical Trapping - Trapping techniques that are applied while standing face to face with your adversary. (See Immobilization Attack).

Viciousness - A combative attribute. Dangerously aggressive behavior. Victim - Any person who is the object of a particular crime.

Visualization - The purposeful formation of mental images and scenarios in the mind's eye.

Visual Monitoring Points - Specific points or locations on your assailant that you should look at during an emergency self-defense situation.

W

Warm-up - A series of mild exercises, stretches, and movement designed to prepare you for more intense exercise.

Weak Side - The weakest and most uncoordinated side of your body.

Weapon and Technique Mastery - A component of CFA's physical component. The kinesthetic and psychomotor development of a weapon or combative technique.

Weapon Capability - An assailant's ability to use and attack with a particular weapon.

Weapon Hierarchy Mastery - Possessing the knowledge, skills and attitude necessary to master the complete hierarchy of combat weapons.

Weapon Uniformity - Gripping and/or drawing your hand-held weapon the same way every time.

Webbing - The first phase of the Widow Maker Program. Webbing is a two hand strike delivered to the assailant's chin. It is called Webbing because your hands resemble a large web that wraps around the enemy's face.

Western Boxing - A Western combat sport that only employs punching-range tools.

Widow Maker Program – A CFA program specifically designed to teach the law abiding citizen how to use extreme force when faced with immediate threat of unlawful deadly criminal attack. The Widow Maker program is divided into two phases or methodologies: Webbing and Razing.

Y

Yell - A loud and aggressive scream or shout used for various strategic reasons.

Z

Zero Beat – One of the four beat classifications of the Widow Maker, Feral Fighting and Savage Street Fighting Programs. Zero beat strikes are full pressure techniques applied to a specific target until ruptures. They include gouging, crushing, biting, and choking techniques.

Zone One - Anatomical targets related to your senses, including the eyes, temple, nose, chin, and back of neck.

Zone Three - Anatomical targets related to your mobility, including thighs, knees, shins, and instep.

Zone Two - Anatomical targets related to your breathing, including front of neck, solar plexus, ribs, and groin.

Zoning - A defensive maneuver designed to negate your assailant's stick strike through strategic movement and precise timing. Zoning can be accomplished by either moving into the direction of your assailant's strike (before it generates significant force) or by moving completely out of his stick's arc

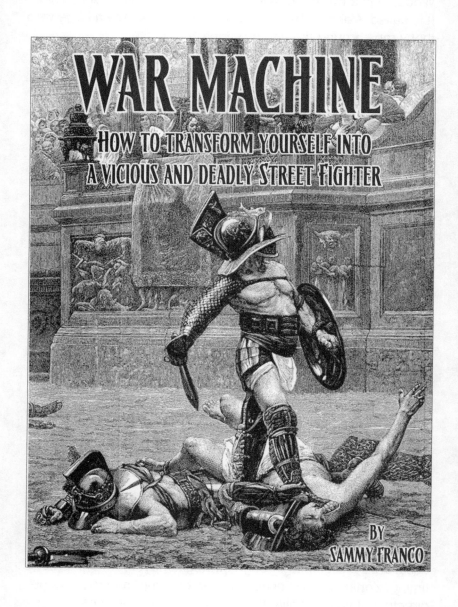

Suggested Reading & Viewing

SUGGESTED READING (BOOKS):

• Boxing Domination: A 21-Day Program to Psych-Out, Confuse, Frustrate, and Beat Your Opponent in Boxing and MMA

• Power Boxing Workout Secrets

• Speed Boxing Secrets: A 21-Day Program to Hitting Faster and Reacting Quicker in Boxing and Martial Arts

• Knife Fighting: A Step-by-Step Guide to Practical Knife Fighting for Self-Defense

• The 10 Best Knife Fighting Techniques

• The 10 Best Power Punches: For Boxing, Martial Arts, MMA and Self-Defense

• The 10 Best Mental Toughness Exercises

• The 10 Best Ways to Defeat Multiple Attackers

• The 10 Best Ways to Develop Your Killer Instinct:

• The 10 Best Bar Fighting Moves: Down and Dirty Fighting Techniques to Save Your Ass When Things Get Ugly

• The 10 Best Sucker Punch Tricks

• Survival Weapons: A User's Guide to the Best Self-Defense Weapons for Any Dangerous Situation

• Knockout: The Ultimate Guide to Sucker Punching

• The 10 Best Kicking Techniques

• The 10 Best Stick Fighting Techniques

• Cane Fighting: The Authoritative Guide to Using the Cane or Walking Stick for Self-Defense

• The Heavy Bag Bible: 3 Best-Selling Heavy Bag Books In One Massive Collection

• Double End Bag Workout

• The 10 Best Things To Do When Held At Gunpoint

• The 10 Best Ways To Defeat Multiple Attackers

• The 10 Best Things To Do During a Mass Shooting

WAR MACHINE II: Real-World Self-Defense Skills for The Warrior Within

- The 10 Best Stick Fighting Techniques
- Bruce Lee's 5 Methods of Attack
- The Widow Maker Compendium (Books 1-3)
- Heavy Bag Workout
- Heavy Bag Combinations
- Invincible: Mental Toughness Techniques for the Street, Battlefield and Playing Field
- Unleash Hell
- Feral Fighting
- Savage Street Fighting
- Stand and Deliver
- The Widow Maker Program
- Maximum Damage
- Kubotan Power
- The Complete Body Opponent Bag Book
- Self-Defense Tips & Tricks
- Heavy Bag Training: Boxing, Mixed Martial Arts & Self-Defense
- Out of the Cage: A Complete Guide to Beating a Mixed Martial Artist on the Street
- Gun Safety: For Home Defense and Concealed Carry
- Warrior Wisdom: Inspiring Ideas from the World's Greatest Warriors
- Ground War: How to Destroy a Grappler in a Street Fight
- 1001 Street Fighting Secrets: The Principles of Contemporary Fighting Arts
- War Machine: How to Transform Yourself into a Vicious and Deadly Street Fighter
- The Bigger They Are, The Harder They Fall: How to Defeat a Larger & Stronger Adversary in a Street Fight
- First Strike: Mastering the Preemptive Strike for Street Combat
- When Seconds Count: Everyone Guide to Self Defense
- Killer Instinct: Unarmed Combat for Street Survival
- Street Lethal: Unarmed Urban Combat

SUGGESTED VIEWING (VIDEOS):

• Combat Energy Drills

• Punching Mitts: Drills & Workout Routines

• Judge, Jury & Executioner

• Pepper Spray: A Video Guide to Using Pepper Spray for Self Defense

• Pressure Points: The Science of Striking Vital Targets

• Sparring: Tips: Tips, Tactics & Techniques to Dominate Your Opponent

• Kubotans & Yawaras: A Quick & Dirty Guide

• Submission Fighting for the Street (Volume 1)

• Submission Fighting for the Street (Volume 2)

• Submission Fighting for the Street (Volume 3)

• Medicine Ball Workout (Volume 1)

• Medicine Ball Workout (Volume 2)

• Double End Bag Training

• Heavy Bag Training

• Power Punching

• Speed Training for Street Fighting (Volume 1): Visual Reflexes

• Speed Training for Street Fighting (Volume 2): Tactile Reflexes

• Speed Training for Street Fighting (Volume 3): Recognition & Auditory Reflexes

• Speed Training for Street Fighting (Volume 4): Movement Speed

• Wrist Locks For The Street (Volume 1)

• Wrist Locks For The Street (Volume 2)

• Choke Out

• Body Opponent Bag Training

• War Machine II

• Sneak Peek

• Armed to the Teeth (Volume 1)

• Armed to the Teeth (Volume 2)

325

WAR MACHINE II: Real-World Self-Defense Skills for The Warrior Within

- Defend or Die
- Escape Master
- In Your Face
- Engage With Rage
- First Strike
- Ground Fighting in The Streets
- Batter Up
- Under The Gun
- Street Stick Fighting
- Use It or Lose It
- Rat Packed
- ,Ground Pounders
- Control & Conquer (Volume 1)
- Control & Conquer (Volume 2)
- Savage Street Fighting: Tactical Savagery As A Last Resort
- The WidowMaker Program: Maximum Punishment for Extreme Situations
- Feral Fighting Program: Level 2 WidowMaker
- War Blade Program: A Complete Guide to Tactical Knife Fighting

About Sammy Franco

With over 35 years of experience, Sammy Franco is one of the world's foremost authorities on armed and unarmed self-defense. Highly regarded as a leading innovator in combat sciences, Mr. Franco was one of the premier pioneers in the field of "reality-based" self-defense and martial arts instruction.

Sammy Franco is perhaps best known as the founder and creator of Contemporary Fighting Arts (CFA), a state-of-the-art offensive- based combat system that is specifically designed for real-world self-defense.

CFA is a sophisticated and practical system of self-defense, designed specifically to provide efficient and effective methods to avoid, defuse, confront, and neutralize both armed and unarmed attackers.

Sammy Franco has frequently been featured in martial art magazines, newspapers, and appeared on numerous radio and television programs. Mr. Franco has also authored numerous books, magazine articles, and editorials, and has developed a massive library of instructional videos.

Sammy Franco's experience and credibility in the combat sciences is unequaled. One of his many accomplishments in this field includes the fact that he has earned the ranking of a Law Enforcement Master Instructor, and has designed, implemented, and taught officer survival training to the United States Border Patrol (USBP).

He has instructed members of the US Secret Service, Military Special Forces, Washington DC Police Department, Montgomery County, Maryland Deputy Sheriffs, and the US

327

Library of Congress Police. Sammy Franco is also a member of the prestigious International Law Enforcement Educators and Trainers Association (ILEETA) as well as the American Society of Law Enforcement Trainers (ASLET) and he is listed in the "Who's Who Director of Law Enforcement Instructors."

Sammy Franco is a nationally certified Law Enforcement Instructor in the following curricula: PR-24 Side-Handle Baton, Police Arrest and Control Procedures, Police Personal Weapons Tactics, Police Power Handcuffing Methods, Police Oleoresin Capsicum Aerosol Training (OCAT), Police Weapon Retention and Disarming Methods, Police Edged Weapon Countermeasures and "Use of Force" Assessment and Response Methods.

Mr. Franco holds a Bachelor of Arts degree in Criminal Justice from the University of Maryland. He is a regularly featured speaker at a number of professional conferences and conducts dynamic and enlightening seminars on numerous aspects of self-defense and combat training.

On a personal level, Sammy Franco is an animal lover, who will go to great lengths to assist and rescue animals. Throughout the years, he's rescued everything from turkey vultures to goats. However, his most treasured moments are always spent with his beloved German Shepherd dogs.

For more information about Mr. Franco and his unique system of self-defense, you can visit his website at: ContemporaryFightingArts.com

COLD INDIFFERENCE DRENCHES MY FACE
AS BLUE HEAVENS TURN TO DUST
I AM BANISHED BY THE HUMAN RACE
FOR MY DARK SOUL CRAVES VIOLENT LUST
OH GRANT ME THIS RIGHTFUL DREAM OF HATE
IN WHICH FLESH AND BONE SEAR WITH PAIN
THE CLOCK TICKS ON UNTIL ITS TOO LATE
AND THOSE WHO OPPOSE ME LIE FALLEN SLAIN

- WAR MACHINE CHRONICLES
CHAPTER XX, VERSE 3

Made in the USA
Middletown, DE
28 October 2023

41544997R00195